Smarter Homes

How Technology Will Change Your Home Life

Alexandra Deschamps-Sonsino

Apress®

Smarter Homes: How Technology Will Change Your Home Life

Alexandra Deschamps-Sonsino
London, UK

ISBN-13 (pbk): 978-1-4842-3362-7   ISBN-13 (electronic): 978-1-4842-3363-4
https://doi.org/10.1007/978-1-4842-3363-4

Library of Congress Control Number: 2018957122

Managing Director, Apress Media LLC: Welmoed Spahr
Acquisitions Editor: Natalie Pao
Development Editor: James Markham
Coordinating Editor: Jessica Vakili

Cover designed by eStudioCalamar

Cover image designed by Freepik (www.freepik.com)

Distributed to the book trade worldwide by Springer Science+Business Media New York, 233 Spring Street, 6th Floor, New York, NY 10013. Phone 1-800-SPRINGER, fax (201) 348-4505, e-mail orders-ny@springer-sbm.com, or visit www.springeronline.com. Apress Media, LLC is a California LLC and the sole member (owner) is Springer Science + Business Media Finance Inc (SSBM Finance Inc). SSBM Finance Inc is a **Delaware** corporation.

For information on translations, please e-mail rights@apress.com, or visit http://www.apress.com/rights-permissions.

Apress titles may be purchased in bulk for academic, corporate, or promotional use. eBook versions and licenses are also available for most titles. For more information, reference our Print and eBook Bulk Sales web page at http://www.apress.com/bulk-sales.

Any source code or other supplementary material referenced by the author in this book is available to readers on GitHub via the book's product page, located at www.apress.com/978-1-4842-3362-7. For more detailed information, please visit http://www.apress.com/source-code.

Printed on acid-free paper

For Marcel

Table of Contents

About the Author

Alexandra Deschamps-Sonsino is an interaction designer, product designer, consultant, and entrepreneur. She was named 1st in a list of 100 Internet of Things Influencers (*Postscapes*, 2016), 2nd in Top 100 Internet of Things Thought Leaders (*Onalytica*, 2014), and among the Top 100 Influencial Tech Women on Twitter (*Business Insider*, 2014). She is the founder of the Good Night Lamp, connected lamps for your global friends and family. She was co-founder and CEO of Tinker London, a smart product design studio. Tinker was the first distributor of the Arduino platform in the United Kingdom. Her work has been exhibited at the Museum of Modern Art in New York, the Victoria & Albert Museum, the London Design Museum, and galleries around the world.

About the Technical Reviewer

Daniel Soltis is a creative technologist and user experience designer living in far northern California. He studied at ITP at New York University and has worked with design and technology companies in London and New York. He has been a technical editor for books on topics including the Internet of Things, Arduino, Raspberry Pi, and Python.

Acknowledgments

This book was made possible with the support of many organizations and individuals.

I'd like to thank the academic and public access libraries around the world, where I wrote large parts of this book, especially the New York City Public Library.

The Institute of Engineers and Technologists Archives team for access to the Electrical Association of Women's work. TechUK for helping me use work from The Setmakers. The Morgan Library for access to their archives. She Runs It for their patience in tracking down the papers belonging to Christine Frederick. Trevor Yorke for his generosity in pointing me in the right direction. David McFayden for his generosity in sharing the Smart House story. Jim Sutherland for his generosity in sharing his pioneering work in home computing. Janet Mobbs for her availability in sharing her and her partner's journey building a Wikihouse. Raven Row gallery for access to their Ulm catalog. The Braun team for access to their collection. Clare Colvin at the Royal Television Society. Otago Polytechnic for the cover art from their alumni Shelley McConaughy. Susan H. Henderson for her work on Marguerite Schutte-Lihotzky. Jean Davis at the New Jersey State Federation of Women's Clubs of GFWC for her help in sharing the history of women experimental homes in New Jersey. Molly Steenson for sharing her work on architecture and computing. To Frank Vukas, Anne Shewring, Josie Dixon, and Claire Selby for their friendship. To Marielle Labrie, Remy, and Marc-André Gauthier for their love. This book is for Marcel Gauthier.

Introduction

Smart homes, as an image, feel familiar yet modern. After decades of science fiction films, the Jetsons and next-generation appliances claiming to solve all our domestic issues, the use of "smart homes" has aligned itself with our collective expectations. Technology has seemingly changed the ways in which we entertain ourselves and others; we eat, restore ourselves, and keep ourselves healthy.

Our commonly developed ideas of home interactions are being disrupted by social media, connected non-screen-based devices (the Internet of Things), e-commerce, the so-called "gig economy," artificial intelligence (AI), chatbots, blockchain, virtual reality, "Big Data," and other software-enabled trends. Middle class and affluent households can now improve their homes with a plethora of new services: controllable plugs, light bulbs that change color on demand, or shopping list or playlist controlled by voice or with a mobile app.

These developments have taken place in the last 5 years but reflect a return in using the home as an accelerator of technology ideas. It would be easy to think of our condition as totally modern in the sense that no one else in time could be living like this, but the resulting behaviors, services, and spaces we are imagining, designing, and prototyping in the labs and research departments of today were sometimes already part of our daily lives more than 100 years ago. Ironically, the concept of the smart home is helping us free ourselves from home-centric economic dynamics. We are slowly reconnecting with communities of small, local entrepreneurship and city-based economies and behaviors of the pre-industrial era.

The middle class home in its current shape in the west hasn't changed since the late 1800s. The home would move its layout really only three times in the past hundred years: the first time to introduce a dedicated bathroom, then separate bedrooms, and finally to point the furniture toward the television.

This is telling of a change in time spent with others in the home. Once the basics of Maslow's pyramid of needs had been resolved and the sanitation of a home was good enough to prevent pest and disease, the next thing to do was to find ways for the home to offer us opportunities for self-fulfillment, creativity, and exploration—especially with new industrialized products as assistants instead of the people we had relied on for so long.

Its layout, what we buy, and where we put it is not only an individual decision nor the result of our personal taste and circumstances. Our homes and how we live in them is the result of the violent intrusion of science, welfare laws, and the industrial and economic needs of the late nineteenth century. Technology, design, architecture, and interior design became tools to help us swallow the pill of social and economic change. In 2017, 80% of Unilever's customers are women,[1] and this is not by accident. Since the home economics movement, the feminist movement, and the post-war boom, the women's place was deliberately designed to be in the home rather than at work or in the city.

Smart homes, as an identifiable term, came to life as "smart house" in a 1984 research consortium financed by the US government and spear-headed by the National Association of Home Builders. The ideas explored by this consortium of corporations in the built environment were very close to what would be commercially available in 2017 but without imagining the subtle but important social and economic changes that the internet would bring. This blinkered view would last throughout the 1980s and 1990s where an era sometimes called "domotics" and often

---

[1] http://www.bbc.co.uk/programmes/b08k1b8p

called "home automation" would stagnate, stuck in the market of the rich and the deluded. Building smart systems management felt like a bigger opportunity for those technologists at the time than to address the difficult home market.

In 2017, we have managed in less than 20 years to change the rhetoric of the "smart home" and take it out of its industrial context to weave a new narrative. In this book we will explore those changes to shed light on the smart home of today and identify exactly where real innovation lies. We will look at how homes have changed to adapt to healthier living conditions; new industrial-centric economies; innovation in lighting, heating, and communication; and how the home has contributed to help build industries outside of its white picket fence.

We will see throughout each chapter how these scientific, industrial, and social dynamics influenced households of the day and how they shape today's view of technology as "helpful." We will look at the role of the design sector and advertising in creating a story of the home as a place where identity, care, and creativity could be expressed. We will identify trends in how companies worked with these sectors to control and dictate to consumers what ambitions they should aspire to have and how technology could help them get there.

Most of the examples in this book relate to the United Kingdom and United States, following their historical roles as leaders in the industrial and military ages of the late nineteenth and early twentieth centuries. That isn't to say nothing unique happened elsewhere, as we will see, but the bulk of the lessons to be learned to help today's businesses and start-ups to understand the home space have blueprints there.

Finally we will examine what happens when conflicting concepts of progress interact at home (financial management, real estate bubbles, and digitally enabled work). In an age of service-based living through companies like Airbnb, TaskRabbit, and Deliveroo, the home must adapt to the demands of our economies, our free time, our social habits, and our financial means.

We have stopped letting the home and, by extension, fast-moving goods companies dictate our interactions within it. A certain consumer dictatorship has ended and a new landscape of opportunity where the home is but one of the places we fulfill our economic and civic duties. 'Kitchen soldiers', as the WWI rallying cry went, we are no more.

CHAPTER 1

Everything Electric

For the modern smart home to exist, it's useful to go back in history and examine the social conditions that made integrating new technologies possible and even desirable. It's also important to look carefully at the types of technologies that have been able to find their way into the home and to question why they have been so successful. It hasn't always come down to technological advances and entrepreneurship, and as we'll see, much of what made the home a trampoline for new technologies was political will and policy-making. We'll start with the heart of the ndustrialization movement: England. British industry, government, and social change contributed to the idea of home life throughout the 1800s, often in parallel. This isn't a small feat. That unique space called the home in turn helped people in cities build a strong identity and relationship to technology.

Historical Background

Between 1820 and 1870, the population of England jumped from 14 million to 26 million[1], with most people living in cities. This was a population made up mostly of "casual agricultural workers"[2] who were going after city-based jobs, bringing with them their livestock. This new population was also made up of younger people receiving their first education. Literacy increased overall in the population from 53% to 76%[3] over 50 years. This was in part due to the Poor Law Amendment Act of 1834 in the United Kingdom, which started almost 100 years of

© Alexandra Deschamps-Sonsino 2018
A. Deschamps-Sonsino, *Smarter Homes*, https://doi.org/10.1007/978-1-4842-3363-4_1

workhouses, industrial schools, and, in more extreme cases, asylums and "Magdalene laundries." Vagrant boys ages 7 to 14 years and pregnant or homeless girls received training for a trade or domestic work. Many would go on to work as servants for affluent families; we will return to their role often across the next chapters.

Victorian working class households lived in squalid conditions. Traditionally five to six family members would share a room of 4 x 4 m. They went out (usually at the back of the building) into an outdoor courtyard to share the use of an outhouse (or "privy") and baths with a larger community. The parents and children all worked in the nearby factories and businesses that were developing, and the time spent at home was limited to getting ready for bedtime.

Eating meant getting a pie or some meat chops from a local "take-away" vendor and cooking it on a "range," which was an iron-cast unit in the middle of which you could light a fire. The unit had plates you could put a kettle on or an iron and a small opening with a door. Cooking at home meant making toast or reheating a soup over this open-fire "range" that was predominantly used for heating the house and drying clothes.

The bulk of city living was about depending on a number of small businesses around you for support and sustinence. For special occasions such as Christmas, you might save up some money and raise a turkey for a few months to slaughter it and have the local "bakehouse" (bakery) bake it for you on Christmas day. On Sundays, American working class families during the same epoch would take a tray of meat and dough on their way to church, drop it by the bakehouse, and pick it up on the way back.[4] The bakers would have used a different seal for each household so they wouldn't give someone the wrong (or smaller) loaf.

Much of life was lived outside the home, which made for easy proliferation of disease. Continual outbreaks of cholera, smallpox, and tuberculosis during the 1830s caused the government of the time to try to legislate not only on how people were working but on how water, waste, and ash were managed in a home.

In 1842 Edwin Chadwick, a social reformer who was one of the architects of the Poor Law, self-published *The Sanitary Condition of the Labouring Population of Great Britain.*[5] He showed the effects of the Poor Law in practice. His descriptions show us the conditions of rural homes of the day:

> *Another cause of disease is to be found in the state of the cottages. Many are built on the ground without flooring, or against a damp hill. Some have neither windows nor doors sufficient to keep out the weather, or to let in the rays of the sun, or supply the means of ventilation; and in others the roof is so constructed or so worn as not to be weather tight. The thatch roof frequently is saturated with wet, rotten, and in a state of decay, giving out malaria, as other decaying vegetable matter.*
>
> *[...]*
>
> *I think there cannot be a doubt if the whole of the wretched hovels were converted into good cottages, with a strict attention to* ***warmth, ventilation, and drainage****, and a receptacle for filth of every kind placed at a proper distance, it would not only improve the health of the poor by removing a most prolific source of disease, and thereby most sensibly diminish the rates.*

His publication led to the subsequent Nuisances Removal and Diseases Prevention Acts of 1848/1849[6] and the Public Health Act of 1875,[7] which forced local governments to take on the financial burden of house waste removal, water purification, and waste management at large. Part of this act banned livestock, made it compulsory for any new building to include indoor toilets or earthclosets (compost toilets) as well as an ash pit on the outside the home to help manage the disposal of ash, and forced local authorities to provide "receptables for the deposit of rubbish."

As a result of this Act, what we know as public infrastructure would start being built. The main limitation of the Public Health Act was that it provided a framework that could be used by local authorities but did not compel action. This meant that city-wide sewage system would take time to be developed, and by the early 1900s many homes still did not have sinks or running water in their kitchens. These changes were not global, and pictures taken in the 1930s and 1940s by photographers Walker Evans and Dorothea Lange in American "'dustbowl" towns depict very similar conditions, showing the rate of progress was concentrated in cities where most of the squalor was observed and documented.

Poorer households parted with their farm animals, moved their "privy" indoors, creating a dedicated bathroom. The growing industrial sector was able to cater to these new household requirements. The use of newly developed "sanitary" materials and construction practices such as enamelware, copper tubing, and gas-powered boilers and, in some cases, flushing toilets would kick off new industries.

The working classes were the most impacted and would benefit the most from the Nuisances Act. The picture for middle class families of the mid-1800s was different.

Victoria middle class families had a different life. They predominantly relied on servants to do most of the domestic work. Those servants lived in austere conditions—initially in the basement and later, with the Nuisances Act, at the back of the house, away from the household and guests but always ready to be called through the famous system of bells on strings.

Because of this reliance on servants, the more affluent households were slow to adapt to the requirements of the Nuisances Act, as they could not understand why a part of the house had to be dedicated to a bath. After all, when they wanted to wash, servants would bring up a tin bath to their room from the "scullery." Water would be heated and poured into the bath, and it would be dragged away when they were done. Money could buy convenience at the time. This is important to think about when contextualizing the perceived "usefulness" of change. The rich did not suffer from as much disease as the poor, so the solution didn't feel relevant to them. Not only that but much of the nitty gritty of household management was kept away from them. Chamber pots were used by the household at night, put out on the doorstep of each room, and emptied by the servants.

Furthermore, servants were hired on the basis of qualities and skills (cooking, discretion, expediency, relationships with city vendors) that were hard to compete with or automate, so doing away with them for an automated sewage or piping system would have been hard to justify.

The most receptive household to changes that were happening both in terms of legislation and also life sciences would be the middle class home. The home was now host to what had previously been communally managed activities where communal labor was involved. Cleanliness and tidiness needed to be put into effect on an individual basis, creating work for the household, with or without servants. The home, which had been a nighttime base for economically productive members of the family, became a space with new tasks and considerations for a literate middle class. Women married to men occupying the new liberal arts professions created by the industrial age (e.g., lawyers, bankers, accountants) were not obligated to work but were unable to afford many servants. This made for a community of educated, literate women who needed support in learning about their new duties, for however long they might practice them (life expectancy in 1841 was around 42 years).[8] Electricity in the home was still decades away, but it would become the ultimate contributor to a growing concern over two home essentials: cleanliness and "home making."

Even if the medical principles that led to public sanitation and waste removal were flawed, they would lead to changes to the home structure that we still live with, as many homes in England still have Victorian-era housing and plumbing.

This was perhaps the last time for a hundred years a government was able to impose action in the home because of its impact on public good. This tension between public and private, which is so political to us now as we start to suffer from worries of Internet use, was at the time a matter of life and death, so supported by most households.

A combination of science and literature would combine to give us the first social communication tool of the modern era: the cookbook.

Developments in the world of science (organic chemistry in particular) and the labor-focused "scientific management" (which would eventually be nicknamed "Taylorism," after Frederick Taylor's work in the Ford factories) would come to influence the way in which technology would be perceived as helping households achieve the healthiest and best environment for their families. This would all come to a head with cooking.

The first modern English-language cookbook, *Modern Cookery in all its Branches*, reduced to a system of easy practice for Private Families,[9] was published in 1845 by Eliza Acton.[10] What made it unique was that recipes included cooking times and a list of ingredients, a novelty but very much of its time. Her book comes out at a time when scientific discoveries such as the measurement of calories (1819–1824[11]), air quality, and air pollution directly relate to or are affected by what happens inside the home. And the homeowner is held in part responsible for the betterment of society through individual actions.

The home becomes a kind of laboratory where new discoveries can be applied and change people's lives and habits. Her book was even re-edited to integrate changes in response to *Animal Chemistry*, a book written by organic chemist Baron Leibig[12] in 1842. This desire to give universal and scientifically driven access to a set of skills only developed by the few would not only lead to the cookbook industry but also developed a framework for a more homogenous idea of what household management skills were required by a homeowner and what broadly made a "home."

Acton's book also included details on why learning to manage a home was essential to the United Kingdom's image as a nation and how it had a broader, social role to play:

> *foreigners have been called in to furnish to the tables of the aristocracy, and of the wealthier orders of the community, those refinements of the art which were not obtained from the native talent. [...] Amongst the large number of works on cookery which we have carefully perused, we have never yet met*

with one which appeared to us either quite intended for, or entirely suited to the need of the totally inexperienced [and] contained the first rudiments of the art, with directions so practical, clear, and simple, as to be at once understood, and easily followed [...]. These will materially assist our progress; and if experienced cooks will put aside the jealous spirit of exclusiveness by which they are too often actuated, and will impart freely the knowledge they have acquired, they also may be infinitely helpful to us, and have a claim upon our grati-tude which ought to afford them purer satisfaction than the sole possession of any secrets—genuine or imaginary—con-nected with their craft.

This type of publication would expand rapidly over the next decades with the publication of other books like *A Treatise on Domestic Economy for the Use of Young Ladies at Home and at School* (1842) and *The American Woman's Home or Principles of Domestic Science: A Guide to the Formation and Maintenance of Economical, Healthful, Beautiful, Christian Home* (1869) by Catherine Beecher.[13]

In *Book of Household Management: A Guide to Cookery in All Branches* (1861)[14] by Isabella Beeton, the part cookbook, part biology and organic chemistry lessons focused on linking theology and morality to duty in the home and, in Catherine Beecher's case, to childcare as well. A woman's place was in the home because there was so much to do and the job was never done.

A more professionalized field of theory would develop from these writings: home economics. It was pioneered by the first woman to graduate with a science and technology degree: Ellen Swallow Richard. She would come to help define the scientific principles and motivations behind daily routines and housework. She was to research air quality, pollution, and sanitation, eventually becoming the first president of the American Home Economics Association.

With the support of scientific studies and developments, the home was fabricated as a sanctuary, separate from the city, commerce, and work—something it had never been before. Once communal, an extension of a family business, it was now privatized, and its state was the sole responsibility of women.[15] It would be core perfect breeding ground for commodities and infrastructure that could help a woman achieve her newfound role. Electricity would come to play a crucial role in supporting these housewives by first latching on to the idea of cleanliness.

The Shift to Electric

Gas had proved to be problematic and costly to implement in a home context initially. In 1823, the founder of the first New York City gas company, Samuel Leggett, had to use his own home to showcase the benefits of lighting your home at night[16] and prove it was safe to do so. Most households still went to bed at dusk, as candles were expensive and often dangerous.

As working class families would come to earn more with the growth of industrialization, they would transition to oil and gas lighting; this consumed oxygen, so each room had to be "aired out" continuously. Electricity would provide a safer, cleaner alternative.

Before it was to bring the outside world inside through radio and television, electricity was able to bring illumination, warmth, and relief from the toil of daily life—especially in a time where homes were dirty and dark, filled with the tar of gas lighting and indoor chimneys. This newly automated process was unparalleled and added fuel to the fire of the home economics movement and, more importantly, the first feminist movements.

The Electro-Magnet Magazine[17] is an example of the ways in which the industry developed in fits and starts. An early attempt to prove the usefulness of electricity, this short-lived publication (there were just two editions in 1840) was published by the American inventor Thomas Davenport. Inspired by the penny press market, which had started in the 1830s, Davenport decided that the best way to showcase his newly developed electric motor was to start a magazine. Underestimating the cost of editorial work and eventually facing the practicality of running the motors turned out to be too much, and the magazine was shut down.

This is typical of the development any technologies in the home: a struggle of finding and selling the best consumer applications so as to justify the infrastructural costs that support the rest of industry.

Unlike the Great Exhibition of 1851, which featured electric telegraphs but nothing for the home owners, the Paris Exposition of 1878 featured eight electric lighting companies that specialized in the home sector.[18] Light bulbs of varying quality and materials started to make an appearance, and the general public was invited to see it as the newest addition to their homes.

That same year, Joseph Swan, who had been working on improving a design for incandescent light bulbs since 1860, obtained a UK Patent (4933) for his invention on November 27, 1880. He demonstrated it publicly and successfully at the Newcastle upon Tyne Chemical Society on January 17, 1879, where Lord Armstrong, a Newcastle industrialist, was present. In 1880, Lord Armstrong would install Joseph Swan's light bulbs in his country home of Cragside, using a water-powered generator, the first in the world (Figure 1-1).

Figure 1-1. *Light bulbs in Cragside, England*

Across the Atlantic, Thomas Edison's labs were hard at work on the same technology. In 1880, Edison and Swan both applied for a US patent, but Edison's was invalidated in June 1883. Edison tried to sue Swan for infringement in the United Kingdom but lost and had to make Swan partner of his Edison British Electric Works company, which was renamed The Edison and Swan United Electric Company and later known to the general public as Ediswan.

Both men took advantage of their connections in high places and of public displays of their technologies to showcase the safety and advantages of their technologies versus gas and oil lighting. In 1881, Edison lit up the home of his investor J.P. Morgan on Park Avenue in New York; that same year, the Savoy Theatre was partly lit up by Swan's light bulbs.

On Christmas 1882, the New York Edison Company vice president, Edward H. Johnson, had specially designed light bulbs made to decorate his Christmas tree. He was living in the first electrified square mile of New York City at the time, in lower Manhattan, where 85 customers were serviced by jumbo dynamos at Pearl Street Station,[19] the first power station that, in turn, powered 400 light bulbs. He invited a journalist to visit him for the occasion, and such was the excitement that in 1894, President Grover Cleveland sponsored some Christmas light bulbs for his Christmas tree[20] in the newly electrified White House (Figure 1-2). Households would have to wait until 1901 before they would become commercially available.

Figure 1-2. *Light bulbs in the White House, 1894*

The market for light bulbs and lighting was booming, leading to the development of professional practice, institutions, and government-sponsored events. The National Conference of Electricians was convened in September 1884 at the Franklin Institute and was the first national convention of electricians in the nation. The American Institute of Electrical Engineers (AIEE) was also founded later that year.

Sponsored by the US Electrical Commission, the Electrical Exposition[21] in Philadelphia was held in Autumn 1884. The exhibits (196 commercial exhibitors and 1,500 exhibits) included the application of electricity on sewing machines. The Edison Electric Light Company showcased their system of house lighting as supplied from a central station.

Light bulbs, which were the predominent application for electricity, became the subjects of comparative studies, not unlike our consumer reports of today. Carl Hering, who was the assistant electrical engineer at the Benjamin Franklin Institute in Pennsylvania, started publishing comparative life tests for incandescent lamps. Initially industry-facing, these types of publications would soon reach consumers through the ever-expanding sector of women's magazines.

Only 10 years after the first light bulbs were commercialized, the Paris Exposition Universelle of 1889 would showcase electricity in its very own category in a section that translates as "Tooling and Processes" within the mechanical industries. "Electric objects" also started to appear in the furniture and accessories section along with appliances and heating elements. It cannot be underestimated how popular these fairs were and how important they were to the public's imagination—especially because of the Eiffel Tower which was built especially for it. That year, 32 million people visited the Exposition in a country of 38 million inhabitants.[22]

In 1893, Carl Hering (who would eventually become President of the AIEE and had become technical editor of *Electrical World* magazine) would publish "A Report on Electricity".[23] This report focused on the growing sector of electrically powered goods and industry, covering lighting, telephony, and telegraphy as well as miscellaneous applications of electricity, which applied to the home space.

The Consequences

Changes in the workforce, coupled with an obligation to stay at home for middle class wives and mothers, created a lot of tension. Job opportunities were everywhere, but a woman's work was decidedly at home, where she would buy goods and services to keep her family safe and clean. Coinciding with the first labor unions formed around 1881 in the US, literature and science fiction played a role in inviting readers to think twice about the benefits of electricity.

It was even then starting to be perceived as a tool for control and restriction of women's potential. Early feminist political action around social reform was starting to develop, a more complete history of which can be found in Dolores Hayden's book *Grand Domestic Revolution*.[24] with '*The Republic of the future*' by Anna Bowman Dodd[25] and '*Looking Backward*'[26] by Edward Bellamy, women authors also illustrated anxieties and worries about the power of emerging technologies.

These anxieties were experienced by women of working or middle class statute, as they didn't have enough money for servants. It would take another 20 to 30 years before the upper classes were to experience the same anxiety, as their relationship with electrification would limit itself to lighting and heating initially. Electrical companies would have to hold on a little while longer before there was any mass market adoption.

End Notes

1. Education in England: a history, Gillard D. (2018)
    `http://www.educationengland.org.uk/history/`
    `chapter02.html`

2. Trevor Yorke, *The Victorian House Explained*
    (Newbury, UK: Countryside Books, 2005) p. 29.

3. Max Roser, *Esteban Ortiz-Ospina, Literacy* (2018)
    `https://ourworldindata.org/literacy/`

4. Valerie Porter, *Yesterday's Countryside: Country Life
    as it Really Was* (David & Charles 2006)

5. Edwin Chadwick, *Report on the sanitary conditions
    of the labouring population of Great Britain.* (H.M.
    Stationery Office, 1843) p. 6.

6. William Cunningham Glen, *The Nuisances Removal
    and Diseases Prevention Acts* (London, Shaw & Sons,
    1849)

7. Public Health Act (1875) `http://www.legislation.`
    `gov.uk/ukpga/1875/55/pdfs/ukpga_18750055_`
    `en.pdf`

8. Office for National Statistics, *How has life expectancy
    changed over time?* (UK, 2015)
    `http://visual.ons.gov.uk/how-has-life-`
    `expectancy-changed-over-time/`

9. Eliza Acton, *Modern Cooking for Private Families
    Reduced to a System of Easy practice* (London, UK,
    Longman, Green, Longman & Roberts, 1860)

10. Tonbridge Historical Society, *Eliza Acton - poet and cookery writer* (2017)
    http://www.tonbridgehistory.org.uk/people/
    eliza-acton.htm

11. James L. Hargrove, *History of the Calorie in Nutrition* (The Journal of Nutrition, Volume 136, Issue 12, 1 December 2006) p. 2957-2961.

12. Eliza Acton, *Modern Cooking for Private Families Reduced to a System of Easy practice* (London, UK, Longman, Green, Longman & Roberts, 1860)

13. Catherine E. Beecher, *A Treatise on Domestic Economy for the Use of Young Women at Home and At School*, (US, Harper & Brothers, 1848)

14. Isabella Mary Beeton, *Mrs. Beeton's household management* (London, Ward, Lock & Co, 1907)

15. Geffrye Museum (London)

16. Hugh Entwistle Macatamney, *Cradle Days of New York* (1909) p. 116-117
    https://todayinsci.com/Events/Technology/
    GasLightingNewYork.htm

17. The Evening Post (New York, 1840) p. 2.

18. Catalogue officiel de Exposition universelle internationale de 1878 à Paris, p. 227

19. Engineering & Technology Wiki, *Pearl Street Station*,
    http://ethw.org/Pearl_Street_Station

20. The White House Historical Association, *Christmas Traditions at the White House Fact Sheet*
    https://www.whitehousehistory.org/christmas-
    traditions-at-the-white-house

21.   Report of the Electrical Conference at Philadelphia in September, 1884 (Washington, D.C.,Government Printing Office, 1886)

22.   Population statistics: historical demography of all countries, their divisions and towns http://www.populstat.info/Europe/francec.htm

23.   Carl Hering, *Electricity at the Paris Exposition of 1889*, (New York, W.J. Johnston Company, 1893)

24.   Dolores Hayden, *Grand Domestic Revolution (MIT Press*, 1981)

25.   Anna Bowman Dodd, *The Republic of The Future* (New York, Cassell, 1887)

26.   Edward Belamy, *Looking backward 2000 to 1887*, (Boston, Ticknor & Co. 1888)

CHAPTER 2

Homes as Factories

Electricity became the engine of much commerce and industrial development at the turn of the twentieth centry—none more lucrative than the war effort. How could households continue to play a role in this landscape? By 1926, 96% of American homes would be electrified,[1] while European homes had to wait for post-war recovery.

The first decades of the twentieth century were key not just in making electricity an agent of improved health but also in turning the home into an extension of what was happening elsewhere in the city, at work in the factory, and eventually at war.

As industrial needs increased, this posed the problem of nighttime efficiency. To afford to run a national energy grid continuously, demand had to be generated for as many hours as possible, including after-work hours. The home became the extension of the industrial age, a necessary actor in the story of industrialization and progress. It was also an opportunity to help industry recoup from the blow of the end of WWI; the use of design, which we'll discuss later in this chapter, became the perfect tool for economic growth in the home sector.

To take up its role in balancing the use of a national energy grid, the use of electricity in the home had to be increase and different arguments had to be used to convince home owners. Electrifying an entire home was expensive for the average middle class home and required a complete change of environment and upgrading of appliances. The endpoints of electricity had to make sense for a household to invest in a complete and

© Alexandra Deschamps-Sonsino 2018
A. Deschamps-Sonsino, *Smarter Homes*, https://doi.org/10.1007/978-1-4842-3363-4_2

expensive retrofit. Barely standardized plugpoints and a new variety of appliances also confused the early middle classes.

The cost of installation as well as the actual cost of the electricity itself would also be a barrier for many decades. Early British installers, backed by local council support, charged households on a monthly basis per power socket that was installed.[2] The scheme also allowed a household to hire appliances such as electric cookers, heaters, and washing machines. In the London borough of West Ham, 572, 792 units were sold in 1900 compared to 74 million in 1927,[3] so these rental models helped homeowners "buy in" electricity at their pace and the pace of their income stream. This was a hard sell nonetheless, and popular culture would play an important role in making an electric home into a necessity and not only a luxury.

The Age of Electrical Conviction

At the turn of the twentieth century, 89% of the US population was literate,[4] and newspapers and magazines offered every industry a new way into people's lives. Convincing a general public to turn their home into the experimental lab of an entire industry took some time, but the tools of conviction were already in place. Methods of persuasion were developing with the early development of the field of psychology. The first advertising agencies offered new approaches, on top of traditional door-to-door salesmen, post contests, parades, and educational fairs.[5]

Advertising turned to film-making, with adverts shown at the start of feature films in the cinemas or between double bills.

General Electric, a merger of Thomas Edison's Edison General Electric Company with Thompson-Houston Electric Company, started to use the newly emerging film and cinema techniques to showcase all-electric homes. "The Home Electrical" is a silent film made in 1915. Set in a middle class home with a black servant using a vaccum cleaner, the lady of the house uses an electric Singer sewing machine, electric bathroom fixtures, and an electrically heated dish and other electrically powered novelty items. Crucially the film ends with "I certainly owe these wonderful conveniences to my wife."

Women were continuing to be targeted and encouraged to feel like the home managers who were responsible for introducing new innovations.

The Electrical Age

In the United Kingdom, the energy sector would do more than invest in advertising to women: they invested in supporting women's work in the electrical sector. *The Electrical Age* was a magazine published by the Electrical Association for Women between 1926 and the late 1970s. Its aim was to introduce all women to the technical wonders of an "all-electric home." In its first edition, R.P. Soan, President of the British Electrical Development Association, provided an introduction and reason for being of the magazine:

"The Electrical Age should act as a much needed link between the women who are studying electricity and its many uses and those who will benefit by its applications, particularily in the home."

There was no acknowledgement, at that point in time, of the industrial forces that needed the average household to buy electrical goods in order to make those industries thrive. This came later. But as a matter of principle, the reason for such a magazine was simply a matter of knowledge-sharing between educated women and the average housewife. The economic argument made by Soan as he introduced the pricing schemes was his only contribution to the magazine.

Every new consumer, so to speak, earmarks for himself a little portion of the whole undertaking and its costs; his annual bill for electricity must cover these charges whether he employs many units or few. A user, perhaps, requiring electric light for only a few hours each evening must, therefore, pay a higher rate per unit than one who also uses power for cooking or driving machinery, which spreads out his demand over many more hours of the day or night.[6]

What is now referred to in industrial circles as demand-side management wasn't an issue at the time, but leveling off the use of the grid was. So the more people used it at night, the more energy companies could invest in growing the grid itself. The publication would not refer strictly to this dynamic elsewhere during its life but would instead feature repeating themes and content. These included how to help households choose appliances to enhance the quality of home illumination. Even in its first edition, interior design and recommendations about shades and fixtures were made to match the quality of gas lighting, deemed more intimate and romantic. Called "lighting schemes," they were meant to be "brought up to date," putting pressure on a household to keep up with the times and fashions. An article, "Light for the Modern Home" is an example of the degree to which language was changing to define rooms in houses.

"The woman of to-day, however 'advanced' she may be, still possesses a good supply of house-pride. [...] Apart from the joy of possession natural to every woman whose home is the centre of her life, there is the ambition to create a home which is not merely a reflection of good taste in the choices of furniture and decorations, but which also gives subtle evidence of the owner's personality. [...] To many housewives the possession of electric light means a form of illumination which, from the point of view of cleanliness and convenience, is a vast improvement on previous methods.[...] The room which more than any other invites the touch of the lighting artist is the drawing-room or lounge. With its multiplicity of uses as a modern living-room, it calls for an illumination which fulfills the requirements of many and diverse occupations."

In 1935, to further convince their readers of the benefit of electricity in the home, the EAW commissioned the furniture and interior design firm P.D. Gane to build an "all-electric home" in Bristol (Figure 2-1). It included:

"6 inset fires, 3 directional fires, 12ft. of tubular heating, 3 electric clocks, 1 linen cupboard heater, 1 towel rail, 1 refrigerator (2 cub.ft. capacity) and 1 fan. Electric cooker and storage heaters for bath and sink supplies on hire. Garden lay-out additional. Running cost for electricity estimated at £30 per annum by the Association."

Figure 2-1. *The Bristol All-Electric Home by the E.A.W*

The idea of electricity as a direct contributor to an "efficient home" was also very much part of the discourse in the December 1926 edition,[7] when Christine Frederick was invited to contribute an article, "How the American Housewife Achieves Leisure through electricity."

> *Badly arranged kitchen vs. Effecient Kitchen*
> *Getting breakfast 45mns vs 20mns*
> *Making Bread 30mns vs 15mns*
> *Holiday Dinner 2h30mn vs 1h20mn*

The kitchen has become a "cheerful, sanitary food laboratory. [T]here is no smell or soot because electricity has superseded coal and ashes; and other portable electric utilities such as the electric mixer, beater, electric tea machine or toaster, etc enable the worker to remain neat and tidy while she does her work with step-saving convenience."

Since the American woman is doing all or most of her own housework, and since even the "new-fashioned" servant when obtainable, refuses to perform the heavy work previously considered as part of her duties,

American builders have been forced to recognise these special conditions. There have been developed, consequently, many excellent designs and models of what we call the "servantless house" or "the self-service house."

It is specifically designed for the woman who herself manages the home or when a single servant only is employed.

Work which formerly required hours of long labour and which caused the dress of the worker to become soiled and insightly, can now be done in 50% or even 20% of the previous time and that by a worker who remains neat and attractive. Household operations, just like those in a factory or plant, may be standardised, simplified, and reduced to a basic time study. The processes of housework are identical with processes and operations in the whole industrial field. In short there is just as much need for "engineering" and "management" in the household as there is in the manufacturing plant.

Christine Frederick was by then a household name in the home efficiency circles, so it's unsurprising she found electrical appliances a positive addition to the household.

Christine Frederick and Domestic Experimental Stations

The founder of the Advertising Women of New York (now known as She Runs It[8]) in 1912, Christine Frederick began to take an interest in her husband's work in Taylorism. She wasn't the only one, and at the time, government grants had produced a community of home owners who were transforming their own homes into "experimental stations" across the US.

The Good Housekeeping Experiment Station[9] had opened in 1900 in New York City, and around the same time Charles and Mary Barnard opened the Housekeeping Experimental Station in Darien, Conneticut.[10] The Barnards published pamphlets and explored effeciency in the home through scientific management techniques. When Charles retired in 1911, Georgie Boynton Child and George Boynton took over and ran the

Housekeeping Bureau of Information, also publishing pamphlets and eventually a book in 1914 entitled, "*The Efficient Kitchen; Definite Directions for the Planning, Arranging and Equipping of the Modern Labor-Saving Kitchen.*"

In 1910 in Colonia, New Jersey, Mary Pattinson opened a State Housekeeping Experimental Station in her capacity as President of the New Jersey's Federation of Women's Club.[11] She published, "*The Business of Home Management (The Principles of Domestic Economy)*" which included an introduction by Frank W. Taylor, father of Taylorism. She later also published "*Principles of Domestic Engineering*" in 1915.

Most of these publications were lost to history unlike Christine Frederick's. Perhaps for no other reason than Frederick was a known writer for the *Ladies' Home Journal*, where she started a column in 1912 entitled "New Housekeeping". She also marketed her ideas through public lectures on the Chautauqua circuit the year her book came out in 1918.[12] She shared with audiences around the country her thoughts on how the emerging field of ergonomics and scientific management could be applied as much to the home as it was to the factory. The Chautauqua and Lyceum circuits were an example of fairs that went around the United States, offering rural areas exposure to the developments in entertainment, science, and technology that were developed across the country. She was key in turning the scientific and science-dependent home of the late 1800s into a factory-like engineered environment where tasks could be accomplished in the most efficient manner.

Years before Le Corbusier would write in *Vers une architecture* "Une maison est une machine-à-habiter" (A house is a machine for living in), Frederick was literally making the home into a machine.

"Replace the unskilled, wasteful and already rapidly dissapearing servant by the use of machinery and household labor-savers. Just as man has revolutionised the farm, factory and office with the tractor and the adding machine, so the time, effort and fuel

required in household tasks can be reduced by 20% to 50% by the use of washing and ironing machines, dishwashers, vacuum cleaners and fireless and pressure cookers, etc. Establish courses in applied mechanics for girls in all schools and college so that the next generation of women will be the masters of labor saving machinery and make it serve them in the home of the future."

She also turned her own home in Greenlawn, New York, into the "Applecroft Home Experiment Station." She applied motion studies to the home, drawing up diagrams of the most efficient layouts for a home, and reviewed thousands of products for various publications.

Published in 1914, Frederick's first book, *Housework Engineering*, was very popular and translated in many languages, helping sow the seeds of some later design and architectural experiments globally. She attempted to seduce, and sometimes guilt, women into taking a positive, engineer-led attitude toward not only housework but home-making in general.

"Woman's vanity has often kept her from admitting that many of her problems are so distressing simply because of her own lack of personal efficiency, not because of circumstances, fate or other people."

She claims in Chapter 12 which was entitled "Developing the Homemaker's Personal Efficiency",

"The end and aim of home efficiency is not the perfect system of work, or scientific scheduling, or ideal cleanliness and order; it is the personal happiness, health and progress of the family."

Her role as a thought leader extended to the space of women's role in the economy at large. In 1929, she published, "Selling Mrs Consumer,"[13] a comprehensive study of women as consumers. In it, she predicts the advent of modern economic tools like the Consumer Price Index, an increase in obesity and a national move away from tradition staples and toward sugary foods.

She also became largely responsible for a degree of consumer acceptance of planned obsolescence, as there was no end to "home-making;" it was endless, the task was never done, never fully accomplished. So vague was the description of home-making, that the image of a better home was taken on board by many women regardless of culture and geography.

Frederick understood that to sell new products for the home, one had to create the social impetus and social conditions for those products to be seen as solutions, or at least helpers, to a problem of better home-making. Talking about it in a scientific way made the pursuit of the right tools a righteous one, however futile. This framework would grease the wheels of the industrial sector across the world for the next century.

Frederick was of course not the only promoter of such approaches. Publications such as the 1917 book *Riflessioni sulla vita. L'anima della donna (Reflections on life. The soul of a woman)* by Gina Lombroso, and the seminal "The Feminine Mystique" by Betty Friedan in 1963 would continue to describe this phenomenon years later.

Design to Sell

Such was the influence of Frederick that in 1926, four years after her book had been translated into German, architect Margarete Schütte-Lihotzky would design a kitchen using her methodology. Named the Frankfurt kitchen (Figure 2-2), it became a design icon in its own right, but its roots undeniably belong to a community of American men and women who published and developed a methodology that could be turned into an act of design. It's easier though to buy into a new kitchen design than it is to learn a methodology, so Schütte-Lihotzky made history.

Figure 2-2. *The Frankfurt kitchen*

Industrial design was there to support the housewife's decision-making in the home by offering solutions that already embodied the principles of scientific management and efficiency. There was undeniably a degree of psychological manipulation required to make women the engine of the industrial re-engineering that took place after WWI, and this cannot be underestimated in our ideas of the smart home of today.

Design as a technique was in its infancy and wasn't defined as an industry in its own right until the 1920 to 1930s, when educational departments started to call a certain approach to engineering and art "industrial design."

The first industrial design course was offered in France by Jacques-Eugène Amengaud in the 1830s at the Conservatoire National des Arts et Métiers (CNAM) and was initially an offshoot of engineering, mechanics, and architecture. It was also described as "dessin industriel," which literally translates as "industrial drawing."

By the 1920s, the likes of Raymond Loewy and the German art school Bauhaus (1919–1933) built a high profile for design that would bridge the arts, and engineering and give it the meaning we now use more commonly.

Art schools, and soon design schools, were very early on involving their students and graduates in working on industrial briefs to help find new solutions and new products for the home. Artists were also involved, and in 1931 artists May Ray and Lee Miller were commissioned by an energy provider to provide them with a series of surrealist photographs promoting electrical appliances.[14]

In January 1959, the London Ceylon Tea Centre showcased "A Room of One's Own," an exhibition on modern living by students of the Royal College of Art.[15]

This trend for using design and art would bring a breath of fresh air to how ideas were developed and communicated. Students like Hans Gugelot and Hans Roericht at the German Ulm School of Design (1953–1958) worked with industrial companies like Braun and Rosenthaler to create innovative designs for radios, turntables, projectors, and more traditional homewares that are still revered as design classics today.

Bigger Homes to Design For

Industrial design's biggest impact was to help the Western world recover from the economic crash of the Great Depression and later on WWII by helping sell households "new and improved" solutions. These were solutions to problems that had been triggered by a real estate boom that produced larger homes and more private spaces, thus bedrooms and by extension more household management.

The size of the average home in the United States more than doubled in the 20th century even if the average size of a family halved (from 4.6 family members per household in 1900 to 2.59 in 2000).[16] See Figure 2-3.

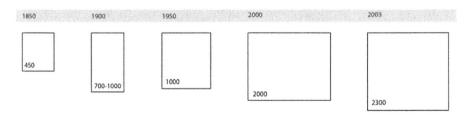

Figure 2-3. *Size of the average American home (square feet) based on M.K. Mason's research*

This negotiation of space and function created new dynamics that could be explored by designers and marketers. The chapter "The Sexual Sell" in the 1957 book *The Feminine Mystique* described these new tensions in the home and how they were resolved through the purchase of new products:

The frustrated need for privacy in the family life' in this era of "togetherness" was another secret uncovered in a depth survey. This need however, might be used to sell a second car. [...] In addition to the car the whole family enjoys together, the car for the husband and the wife separately—"Alone in the car, one may get the breathing spell one needs so badly and may come to consider the car as one's castle, or the instrument of one's reconquered privacy" or "individual" "personal" toothpase, soap, shampoo.[17]

Betty Friedan had been invited to view reports on a variety of consumer products and women's experience of the home. One such study of the "psychology of housekeeping" made in 1945 with a sample of 4,500 middle class college-educated women found 51% of them to fit "The True Housewife" profile, while the rest was split between "The Career Woman" and "The Balanced Homemaker."

By the mid-1950s, "Career Woman" had been replaced by the "less worldly and sophisticated" woman, whose activity in PTA meetings gave her broad contacts with the world outside her home but who found in housework a medium of expression for her femininity and individuality.

Jobs were not a priority, but home-making was a way to reward husbands for their valor in WWII.

They could purchase products that made housework feel "technical" and "complex" like the women to whom Christine Frederick spoke to 40 years prior.

Beyond effeciency howeber, a new concept emerged in design and marketing worlds, that of the "home of the future," which pushed ideas of effeciency and scientific management aside to be replaced by a more inspirational conversation with consumers.

End Notes

1. David E. Nye, *Electrifying America* (Cambridge, MA: MIT Press, 1992), p. 261.

2. *The Electrical Age*, (London, Electrical Association for Women, 1927) p. 227

3. *The Electrical Age*, (London, Electrical Association for Women, 1927) p. 228

4. Max Roser, *Esteban Ortiz-Ospina*, Literacy (2018) https://ourworldindata.org/literacy/

5. David E. Nye, *Electrifying America* (Cambridge, MA: MIT Press, 1992), p. 265

6. *The Electrical Age* (London, Electrical Association for Women, 1926) Volume 1, p. 17

7. *The Electrical Age* (London, Electrical Association for Women, 1926) Volume 1, p. 98–99

8. She Runs It, Our Story (New York City, NY 2018) https://sherunsit.org/who-we-are/

9. Good Housekeeping, The History of the Good Housekeeping Institute (2018) http://www.goodhousekeeping.com/institute/about-the-institute/a17940/good-housekeeping-institute-timeline/

10. Lisa M. Tucker, The Labor-Saving Kitchen: Sources for Designs of the Architects' Small Home Service Bureau (ARCC Journal, 2014) p. 52–63

11. *"Experiment Station to solve housekeeper's problems."* (New York Times, NY: March 26, 1911) p. 56

12. Lisa M. Tucker, The Labor-Saving Kitchen: Sources for Designs of the Architects' Small Home Service Bureau (ARCC Journal, 2014) p. 52–63

13. Selling Mrs Consumer, Christine Frederick (New York, NY: The Business Bourse, 1929)

14. MetCollects, Electricite by Man Ray (New York City, NY: The Metropolitain Museum of Art, 2014) Episode 12 http://www.metmuseum.org/art/online-features/metcollects/man-ray-electricite

15. *The Electrical Age* (London, Electrical Association for Women, January 1927) Volume 11, No. 3.

16. Frank Hobbs and Nicole Stoops, Demographic Trends in the 20th Century (US Census Bureau, 2002) https://www.census.gov/prod/2002pubs/censr-4.pdf

17. Betty Friedan. *The Feminine Mystique*, (New York, NY: Norton, 2001), p. 225.

CHAPTER 3

Pleasure and Convenience

By the end of WWI and during the interwar period, the commercialization of new additions to the home would bring in new ways of interacting with information and entertainment: the radio, dedicated music players, and the television would come to define leisure and convenience, adding to the notion of effeciency. The telephone would additionally give homeowners the ability to negotiate this newfound leisure time alone or with others. Guy Debord's "society of the spectacle" was being built thanks to new technologies in the home space.

From Effeciency to Pleasure

With a growing understanding of human psychology and the growth of the advertising sector with its so-called "persuaders," it became clear that it was going to be much easier to sell chocolate than to sell aspirin, as the saying goes. Convenience and pleasure would be the key arguments to help companies sell new emerging technologies in the home space.

Convenience would stem from helping simplify tasks: to make them easier to take on or easier to understand. Simplification was the complete reverse of the factory age, where actions in the home had to be measured and become more efficient. Convenience was about not having to measure

© Alexandra Deschamps-Sonsino 2018
A. Deschamps-Sonsino, *Smarter Homes*, https://doi.org/10.1007/978-1-4842-3363-4_3

at all because the product did it all. Or if it didn't do it all, it did it better than a person could anyway, no matter how the job was done.

The second concept of pleasure would come in as the excitement of city life was sold to households in suburbia. A communal experience lived in the city could now be offered in the comfort of one's own home, without having to leave the house! The gramophone, radio, and television would take their place in the living room and soon enough in bedrooms and kitchens across the home.

This was ideal to fully occupy the newly earned evenings and weekends after almost a century of grueling round-the-clock factory work.

To make sure the most could be made of this time of pleasure and leisure, one had to make sure one was going to be home alone long enough to enjoy it, so coordinating the comings and goings of the family and others became an essential part of daily life. The telephone would solve that problem soon enough, finally closing the door that had once been often opened by visiting neighbors and vendors.

Thus the modern home was designed, drawn and defined. In this chapter we will look at the development of these technologies and how they came to define how we think of the 1930s to 1950s home.

Out of Sight and Out of Mind

The industrial age and its working conditions was rather punishing for families and gave them very little time together or collectively to enjoy the fruits of their labor. The First World War was brutal, and after a change in labor practices meant parents and children had more time—weekends even—to tinker, entertain themselves, or educate themselves. The factory work of the war was put aside and with it an image of the home as an extension of work. Families could start to work to live.

Modern art and modernism movements in architecture reflected that desire for leisure by developing interiors and buildings using concepts of simplicity, abstraction, cleanliness, and purity. This was the "modern home", and images started to trickle through to home owners by publications and tradeshows.

In 1925, Le Corbusier built the "Pavillion de l'esprit Nouveau" at the Paris Exposition des Arts Decoratifs exhibition.

Described as a "cell-unit,"[1] and the furniture around it as "equipment," it called for precision in human tasks. This was still using the same language of efficiency, but products were starting to dissapear from view. Convenience and pleasure were experienced by removing both dirt, wires, and the sight of servants. The "mechanics" of home-making were in the way of reflection, relaxation, and enjoyment—the new pleasures of post-WWI middle class living.

E-1027

Another example is the work of Eileen Gray. Born in Ireland and trained in London at the Slade School of Art, Gray worked as an interior and furniture designer running her own gallery in Paris. At age 49 years, she designed the structure, interiors, and furniture of a French Riviera villa for her lover, the architect and critic Jean Badovici. She named the summer home E-1027. Badovici was also the curator of "l'Architecture Vivante," one of the earliest quarterly publications dedicated to modern architecture.

Built between 1926 and 1929, E-1027 was a showcase not only of the latest technologies but also the latest thinking in terms of space and what home living represented. Gray would be the one of the first to use cold-pressed steel in her furniture., She treated electrification as a feature, grouping the electric cables as they ran along the walls, playing to the seaside aesthetic of the apartment on the Mediterranean. She also designed a "portable" phonograph to make it possible to enjoy music outside on the generous outdoor veranda and sundecks. Most of the furniture was open in its use, and many hinges and movable panels allowed the spaces to become "other" and hide their primary function.

A cross between a camping experience and that of living on a boat, E-1027 showed us how the nitty gritty of home living should be tucked away, to make place for the living room and communal experiences as much as possible.

The kitchen, the most problematic for a pioneer who was also a woman, was completely out of view. The main entryway to E-1027 had a stenciled "Sens Interdit" on it (or "No entry"). This was the way to the kitchen and the servant's quarters (Figure 3-1).[2] This forbidden corridor lead to the kitchen and then past it, to the servant's room that had a small sink but no toilet. A small bathroom was adjacent with access to an outdoor shower. The bedroom was described in an interview Gray and Badovici penned on the special edition of "L'Architecture Vivante" as "la plus petite cellule habitable," or "the smallest livable cell."

When the publication's photographer came to visit the house to take pictures to support the article, it was the only room not photographed. The kitchen featured obtusely to focus on the storage units, and there was not an ice box nor stove in sight. The message was clear, in an ideal, modern house, cooking wasn't even acknowledged, and every effort was made to hide away.

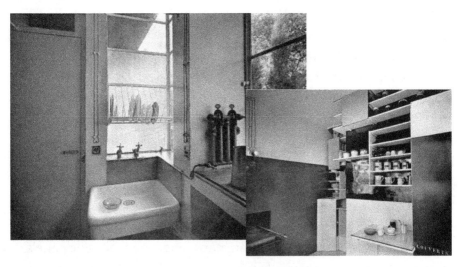

Figure 3-1. *Photography of E-1027's kitchen in l'Architecture Vivante*[3]

What E-1027 developed was an idea of luxury associated with the discreet intervention of technology. Radios were embedded in every room; heating and storage were embedded in the surface of the walls.

This new approach would influence the expectations of households everywhere as modernism's messages permeated advertising, magazines, tradeshows, and expos for decades to come. It would shape how appliances were developed, as highlighted by a survey General Electric (GE) conducted about their refrigerators in 1932.[4]

"Customers 'would rather not have the mechanical part of the device in evidence [...] with respect to complaints that she had heard from other women.' The machine itself is the very thing that the woman buying it wants to keep out of sight and out of mind."

The Kitchen's at the Back

In its approach, E-1027 represented also the limits of an intellectual elite that wanted to move beyond the past formally and aesthetically but continue to retain the advantages of servants.

This blind spot was exposed when that elite would lose access to their servants. The book *America's Kitchens*[5] detailed this through the experience of the Gropius household when they moved to their home in Lincoln, Massachusetts.

Walter Gropius, the first director of the Bauhaus, had designed the house for his family in 1937 after their move to the United States (Figure 3-2). He had designed a kitchen at the back for their maid, Gertrude Ernst. When Gertrude left to take up a factory job, Ise Gropius, his wife, started to cook for the first time in her life. She complained that the kitchen design had been a "mistake,"[6] as it was too far away from the action of the dining room, where guests were being entertained by her husband. The needs of a hostess and a live-in cook were completely unrelated. One had to be kept away, the other was the center of attention.

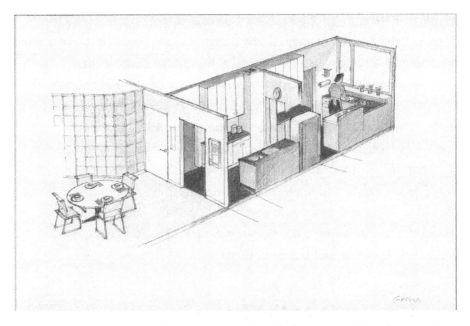

Figure 3-2. *Drawing of the Gropius family home with kitchen at the back*

While the home was turning into an extension of the bathroom—clean, shiny, and bright—other objects were demanding a new kind of attention. There was no name for them initially, and they found their place in the living room. This category of home appliances was completely "other." We would come to call them "devices," a mixture of old French "devis" (which means "to divide") and the fourteenth century meaning of a mechanical contraption.

The home of the 1920s was being exposed to a completely new category of products and behaviors that would not so much change the tasks that had to remain "domestic" but change the interaction between people living in a home and a community of others and information outside the home. These initially screenless devices would move from the living room to permeate the rest of the home space. In the next sections, we will look at the history of the gramophone, the telephone, the radio, and the television—new types of technologically enabled behaviors that brought the outside world in while allowing us to physically close the door on others.

Listening In and Restricting Access

The impact of the telephone and the radio on the home was that they both replaced a communal experience of the city and the home with the ability to pick and choose when one would leave the house and interact with others.

Before the telephone, the front room was a space that received guests on a more-or-less random basis. People dropped by to give you the latest news, for business affairs, or for a bite to eat. A household had to keep themselves rather well-stocked to accommodate strangers and friends at any time. The telephone meant that interactions within the home could be controlled and people could be kept at bay. Entertainment could be purchased and consumed in the home with the phonograph but then could come freely distributed with the radio along with national news. The door could be closed and the front room was changed into a "living room," where a family would enjoy the fruits of the radio and eventually the television together.

These objects replaced the fireplace but also brought the world in, exposing people to music from around the world and news from beyond their own town and borders. Not only that, but someone could "virtually" come in and be trusted to tell you what was important.

These were products the utility of which was so new and unique they did not have to suffer the plight of appliances and "disappear." They were trophies of social mobility and were showcased proudly, especially as industrial design techniques improved and new materials like plastics were developed.

The Sonnenveld House in Rotterdam was an example of this slow intrusion of technology in the dwelling of the rich. Built for the Sonneveld family in 1933, it contained two external phone lines (one in the bedroom and the other in the office) and a system of intercom telephones across the house for family members to call each other or the staff. Only 1 in 25 residents had a telephone at the time in Rotterdam, making this still quite a luxury.[7] In the bedrooms, the wireless radio set was integrated into the bed furniture, not unlike in E-1027 and the Lawn Road flats in London, which we'll discuss later. The furniture and fixtures were designed by Gispen, a pioneering industrial design firm in Rotterdam inspired by Gray's tubular furniture in E-1027. If the rich had been slow to adopt electrification in the late 1800s, they were the first ones to enjoy putting social barriers between themselves and others with the power of architecture and new technologies.

Listen Up

By 1929, the year Grey finished building E-1027, the gramophone was a fixture in most homes. Gray even designed a table to move what looked like a hand-cranked HMV 109 around so guests could listen to music outside from the solarium or garden. Battery technology was improving, and electrification of housing increased the likelihood of new entertainment-based products to be purchased.

Invented by Emile Berliner, a German-born accountant turned inventor who had moved to America in 1870. Berliner was interested in developing ways to transmit and record sound. In 1877, he patented the gramophone, and in 1894 with some financial backing he started a company to manufacture and market 7-inch records and a hand-propelled machine.

Gramophones initially took off as a publicly accessible service. By the late 1890s, so-called "phonograph parlours" were very popular, and people would line up and pay to listen to a piece of music, news, comedy, or whatever other content they liked. If they wanted to have free access, they would have to listen to a minute of advertising demonstrating an early version of the digital "freemium" model.

Because it functioned mechanically, the gramophone rapidly found its place in homes that didn't already have electricity. Working with Eldridge R. Johnson, an engineer based in New Jersey, Berliner worked out how to power the turntable with a cheap, small, spring-loaded motor so such an electrified product could play a disc on its own. Berliner managed to sell 1,000 gramophones and 25,000 records in 1893.[8] Sales of records went from $4 million in 1900 to almost $30 million in 1910. An industry was born.

It would be easy to think that records were an obvious solution to playing music, but for some, like Thomas Edison, the idea that the home setup had an influence on what could be successful was a difficult concept to swallow, especially from someone so successful at coming up with successful inventions. Edison had invested in cylinders as a means to record audio instead of discs, but discs were easier to stack in a bookshelf. This seems like a detail, but design history is littered with product ideas that were unable to fit into the physical fabric of the home. A homeowner will allow a certain degree of sacrifice, but radical change in a domestic setting is rare and costly. By 1919, Edison dropped cylinders entirely and left the music business altogether in 1929.

Initially very bulky, gramophones were sold in furniture stores. Designers tried to emulate Victorian furniture in helping contain the components of the gramophone, but as miniaturization and speaker technology would develop, size would decrease and portability would increase, a trend that radios and telephones would follow, and this would lead to dedicated retail experiences.

Listening In

After WWI, what we nowadays refer to as "tinkerers" or hobbyists were the returning soldiers who had used the first radio systems. Self-assembly radio kits[9] were sold and consisted mostly of wires, valves, and a rather leaky battery. Initially serviced by bicycle shops who had the equipment, it was predominently a male-dominated hobby, and there was no content to listen to.

To be able to broadcast, an amateur radio enthusiast had to get a license from the Post Office but didn't necessarily need one to receive a signal. They also needed headphones to receive a signal, as amplifiers had yet to be invented. In 1904, The United Kingdom's Wireless Telegraphy Act granted control of radio waves to the General Post Office, who licensed all senders and receivers.

Solutions were developing rapidly in the United Kingdom, where cottage industries across the country started working on solving the problems around radio components and batteries. The valves necessary for the development of a radio set were developed in France and by 1916 were manufactured in Britain at the Ediswan lamp factories, as the valves resembled little lamps. In early 1920, the Marconi Company began transmitting speech from Chelmsford to test out long distance propagation,[10] and by June 15, 1920, Dame Nellie Melba gave a 30 mn recital sponsored by the *Daily Mail* owner Lord Northcliffe. Back in the United States, Dr. Frank Conrad, an engineer of Westinghouse's Pittsburgh plant, had set up an amateur radio transmitter and organized so-called "Air concerts."

By 1926, these on-air classical recitals by these early, often self-made celebrities (e.g., Jessica Dragonette) became a fixture of radio. In 1924 Eric Cole and William Verrells developed a battery eliminator, which meant that the radio could eventually be mains-powered.

Again, the ability for a product to connect to the growing and ubiquitous electric network meant more power and more functionality. They formed E.K. Cole Ltd., which would become a leading manufacturer of the most novel radios of the day.

Just as the refrigerator's parts had to be hidden away from sight, the radio's parts had to be encased and ideally looked like any other piece of furniture around while still retaining some uniqueness, following in the footsteps of the gramophone.

The relationship to plastics would become ambivalent after WWII, as people initially wanted to return to "genuine materials"[11] but the American aesthetic, which we'll cover in the next chapter, soon made plastics more desirable.

Pioneering the use of plastics and Bakelite, E.K. Cole hired the architects Wells Coates and Serge Chermayeff to design new enclosures using this new material. Although Chermayeff's Ecko AC-74[12] was, by modernist standards, beautiful (it even came with tubular steel legs similar to Gray's furniture in E-1027), it was Wells Coates's model that turned out to be a commercial success (Figure 3-3).

Figure 3-3. *Advertisement for the Ecko AD-65 by Wells Coates*

The Ecko AD-65 was the first round Bakelite radio on the market, a complete departure from the square wooden boxes that were designed to blend in with cabinets and drawers. As all-day programming was building up to include drama, news, as well as music, the whole family could gather around this totemic object, which was often sold with a pedestal (Figure 3-4).

Figure 3-4. *Family getting together after their dad built a radio kit in 1930*

In the face of growing competition from the Netherlands, Germany and the United States dedicated fairs and tradeshows organized to promote these new products and Britain's industrial prowess. The 1925 "All-Wireless British Show" at the Horticultural Hall was followed by the 1926 "Radiolympia," which ran until after WWII and was so popular even Queen Anne paid a visit.

Households got accustomed to the leisure of being able to listen to music and the news from the comfort of home, and they were next going to change the way they interacted with their community.

Hanging Up

The telephone would introduce a new way to define who is and isn't welcome in our homes and how they may access it. From an industrial point of view, the telephone's development wasn't as closely aligned to the radio, as there was no way to use the network without building it. A novice or "bottom-up" approach that worked for radio sets wasn't possible here. For that reason, the incubation period of the telephone was very long but still tied to a home context.

Before Alexander Graham Bell's patents were developed, many others were trying to extend the utility of telegraphy. One of the first prototypes of a "talking telegraph" was made by Antonio Meucci, an Italian engineer and self-made inventor living in New York's Staten Island. He was interested in the idea in 1849 and started to document his research. By 1854, his wife had become chronically ill with rheumatoid arthritis. In 1856, he used an electromagnetic telephone as a way of connecting his second-floor bedroom to his basement laboratory, thus being able to communicate with his wife.

Between 1856 and 1870, Meucci developed more than 30 different kinds of telephones on the basis of this prototype. His inability to find financial backers meant he had to sell everything in the process of going bankrupt. There were, as with Edison & Swan, intellectual property issues that prevented him from building a telephonic empire. His 1871 caveat (a statement of intent to file a patent) was never turned into a patent, unlike Bell's research and patent of 1876.

Meucci's story isn't unique, as many other developments that would change the face of our interactions with others would come from identifying opportunities in the home space. However, to be able to withstand the intellectual property battles and negotiate with competitors, you had to be well-financed or well-connected. Meucci was neither and didn't speak English.

The first telephone installation in the United Kingdom was in Plymouth by Bell. He was lecturing there in 1877 when he stayed at the residence of Robert Bayly. Bayly's wife felt nervous about living in such an isolated property, so Bell rigged up a telephone line between the main house and the gardener's cottage, one of many "firsts" in the UK for the telephone.[13]

In January 1878, the first US telephone line and switchboard were built, and the first commercial telephone exchange was in operation in New Haven. By the end of the same year, the London & Manchester telephone exchange companies (the first in Europe) were set up. Three years later, almost 49,000 telephones were in use,[14] and by 1900 there were 600,000 phones in Bell's telephone system.

In the United Kingdom, the first public telephone exchange opened in 1879 with just eight subscribers.[15] In 1899, Parliament agreed that local councils could set up their own telephone systems. Only 6 out of the 1,300 councils took advantage of this. By 1912, Britain's first public automatic exchange opened in Epsom, Surrey. For the first time, customers could make calls without going through an operator—the first step toward automation. Just because the network was growing didn't mean that households had access to it. The first functional rotary home phone not plagued by technical problems was the 1930 West Electric 202 model (Figure 3-5).

Figure 3-5. *Western Electric 202 rotary phone*

Manufactured for only 7 years, it was so popular customers still had them until the 1950s when the 500 model took over and sold millions (Figure 3-6).

Figure 3-6. *Western Electric 500*

Many homes around the world still use this model, which was based on the 1931 design of the Ericsson DBH 1001 model by Norwegian designer Christian Bjerknes and fine artist Jean Heiberg.[16] The choice of these two professionals mirrored the choice that Cole made of working with architect Welles Coates. Working with creative people at that time would create shapes that became icons and iconic objects in our homes.

The telephone's amazing growth allowed households to gain a level of autonomy away from their communities but also, hand in hand with the radio, allowed the home to become a place where time could be sent really in complete privacy and comfort. If you hadn't organized any meetings, people would be less likely to knock at the door to see if you were there, as they had before. If you didn't want to be disturbed, you took the phone "off the hook," an expression relating directly to the physical elements of early phones.[17]

This "hookless" design made out of Bakelite would have been cheaper to make than the older models, which would have lead to savings for homeowners getting their first-ever home telephone. It was known around Europe afterward as the "Swedish type of telephone."

Companion Objects

The United Kingdom's version of that phone, the 332 was licensed by the General Post Office and manufactured by British Ericsson, ATM, GEC, Siemens Brothers, and others.[18] Its 1937 version included a small drawer. This seemingly small detail points to the increase in time spent on the telephone. Just like the radio had its stand, the telephone would create its own ecology: new "partner objects."

The year after the Ericsson DBH 1001 was produced, Italian design firm Zanotta created a tubular steel stand for both the phone and telephone directory underneath (Figure 3-7).[19]

Figure 3-7. *Chichibio telephone stand*

Others went further, and the "gossip chair" was born. A chair with an attached raised table and drawer, the only function of that piece of furniture was to cater to the notionally portable experience of the telephone, which in fact meant long conversations, note-taking, magazine reading, and eventually looking up numbers as telephone operators were phased out.[20]

Much later, in 1958, further steps toward "freedom" came when the Subscriber Trunk Dialing (STD; or the ability to make long-distance calls without the help of an operator) was launched by the Queen with a call to Edinburgh. The telephone then became a private transaction, a negotiation, between two unidentifiable parties.

Identifying and finding the other party wasn't a case of knocking on doors but having the right number. The phone directory became the first physical companion to a completely intangible interaction and the first home database. It was able to create a map for a community that was no longer defined by personal interactions but by how bold their name was or whether they'd bought advertising space. It was, in fact, an extension of the newspaper experience.

In 1914, 1.5 million copies were produced in the United Kingdom by a mix of vendors such as BT, the Post Office Telecommunications, and the National Telephone Company, making it the largest single printing contract. By the time the 1937 G.P.O. Film Unit documentary 'Book Bargain' was produced,[21] the London-only directory was 2,500 pages thick and went out to 850,000 subscribers four times a year, to keep up with as the updates and additions required. By 1951, 8 million copies were printed every year.

In total, 1,780 British phonebooks were released between 1880 and 1984,[22] which is an average of 17 books a year. These were often issued in bundles of three to four to accomodate printing methods and paper quality.

By 1948, 30 million phones were connected in the United States; by the 1960s, there were more than 80 million phone hookups in the United States and 160 million in the world; by 1980, there were more than 175 million telephone subscriber lines in the United States.

The gossip chairs and stands of the radio and telephone would help increase the enjoyment of the consumption of both products and would be the last such "companion" products. The same trend that would impact kitchens was moving into the living room, as the television emerged and its presence was "managed" to hide it out of view. This situation still exists now, where the router is often hidden away in a cupboard. As they increased in popularity, devices became mundane, not as worthy of our attention as they had once been. This may have been due to a lack of enthusiasm from the industrial design sector but may also have been explained by the desire to forget what that technological "magic" was actually made of: cables. As more complex objects entered our homes, it wasn't important to know how to repair them or how they actually worked. And none were as complex and as life-changing as the television.

Turn It On

The epitomy of pleasure and entertainment came into the home just on the cusp of WWII. The television came in quite late compared to the rush of radio and the telephone during the 1920s and early 1930s. The home was ready though, as the living room had adapted to the communal pleasures of radio dramas and the news. The television would quickly oust the radio as the focus of the room and still does today. Its presence relied heavily on the growth of radio first, as adding a moving image seemed like a natural enhancement to the experience of listening to someone speak. People were used to going to the theater and seeing silent films, so the meeting of radio and theater would have seemed natural. The home context was unusual, however, and in the United Kingdom, the General Post Office had to reassure the general public that television would not enable others to look into their homes—a fear that will be revisited almost 100 years later with the ubiquitous cameras in our computers and phones.

Philco would sell projection televisions (one of the three ways you could view the screen) as a way of getting "your own theater in your own home."[23] This idea of accessing a communal experience at home comes back with every new technology.

Many "firsts" in the development of the television took place between 1935 and 1938, but the quality of output of the image and the sound would vary until well into the 1970s.

The complexity of choosing a stable method of displaying a picture slowed down manufacturing, affordability, and access. *The Setmakers*, a book published by BREMA in 1991, detailed the various conundrums engineers and the broadcasting industry had to resolve before television was a commercial success. Advertisement was a major point of contention, and faliability of the sets pre- and post-WWII in the United Kingdom were constant battle.

John Logie Baird, a Scottish inventor, had developed what could be considered the first "low-definition" television[24] in London. He demonstrated it in Selfridges in 1925 and then in his Soho office to the press in 1926. Called the "Televisor," it cost between £20 to £150,[25] and early adopters were told that orders would be fulfilled when the broadcasting service was available.

After much hesitation, the BBC allowed transmissions from Baird's South London office to take place outside of normal broadcasting hours, then more regularly from September 30, 1929.[26] Initially Baird's company imagined that 29 sets might be sold and really just wanted to license the right to manufacture it to someone else. Sales were so slow, Baird paid Plessy, a local manufacturer, to produce some sets as well as kits for 16 guineas. Self-assembly kits were available in the United Kingdom for television, just as they had been for radio, but the process was far from simple for a layperson.[27]

It's believed only 1,000 were produced, and only 500 had been sold by December 1932.

This early version of the television depended on a "Nipkow disk" (patented in 1884), which made it easy to use as part of a DIY kit but only produced a resolution of 30 flickering lines. It was quickly superseded by experiments with a mirror drum mechanism (invented in 1889), which produced an image of 9" x 4".

EMI at the time were working on a "high-definition" model, and the BBC was advised in January 1935 to begin an experimental service to support 240 lines of resolution. Excitement quickly grew for these experimental units and service.

In 1937, a 405-line standard was agreed to make sure early adopters didn't invest in something that would become immediately defunct. By June 1937, only 1,500 had been sold across all manufacturers. Radio shops and department stores ran demos of the sets, and there were two sets on the concourse at Waterloo station and in the Science Museum.[28] By 1937, only half of retailers had decided to start selling televisions, which at that stage could be leased for a pound a week.

The 1937 "Radiolympia" tradeshow featured international manufacturers and their new models. Philips had developed a "projection set," as the image was reflected on a mirror on the lid of the unit for the viewer to see and, as a result, could produce a much larger image, at 12". The early sets had screens that were disapointingly small, as the whole family couldn't really cram themselves in a round 9" screen.

The BBC's programming improved and finally sales rose in the last quarter of 1938, to 5,000 sets. By the start of WWII, 18,999 sets are believed to have been sold in the United Kingdom. Sales were then shut down for 7 years, a period during which the American and German markets would grow, as they were able to take advantage of war-time developments and apply them to the post-war models. New models were exhibited at the last pre-war "Radio Show" fair but were never marketed.

In 1939, US sales of televisions to homeowners represented 88.9%, but only 2,000 sets were sold. At the time, the commercial success of television was hard to predict,[29] but by 1952, 34.2% of the US population had one: a decade later, this rose to 90%.

The impact of American content was such, especially for cartoons and children's content, that when the BBC's television program kickstarted again after WWII, it was a 1939 Mickey Mouse cartoon that was shown again.

The first ad aired in 1941 in the United States, promoting a clock company, but it wouldn't be until 1955 that advertising would be allowed on UK national television due to the non-commercial nature of the BBC.[30] It was also due to slower sales, as families had other priorities in the immediate post-war aftermath.

Companies also had to completely re-adapt themselves to a consumer market after being solely focused on military contracts. During the war, households that had invested early in radios and televisions got them fixed, which worked until the materials necessary for repairs were unavailable (including batteries).

The Netherlands-based Philips would pioneer printed circuit boards in television in 1955,[31] helping reduce material and labor costs significantly. Products would slowly miniaturize and get cheaper and better, but the tone was set pre-WWII in the factories of England, across the entire country. The combination of the telephone, the radio, and the television had already made its mark in people's imaginations; they just had to wait a little before being able to afford it.

These have ultimately acted as anchor technologies, to be either rendered more efficient or less visually imposing but still present and demanding our attention.

The impact of telephony, regardless of the slow death of the landline, had been to close the front door of the house in ways that had not been available before. The radio and the television brought in the rest of the world while that door was still closed.

This creation of a controlled private space where entertainment was still available defined our image of privacy. Privacy didn't have to mean isolation; it could mean pleasure and convenience. It was something to aspire to for decades to come and an idealized situation during and immediately post-war when much communal living and communal thinking was done. The telephone, radio, and television came to rescue us from others.

Away from Others

While we've talked about pleasure and convenience in fairly suburban contexts, cities were also creating the conditions for serviced apartments aimed at young working professionals who used technology in very different, sometimes communal ways.

Apartment hotels were common in the late 1800s in cities across America, offering bedsits to young, unmarried, white collar professionals. In Paris they would be called "la chambre de bonne" and were often in the attic. Apartment hotels often focused on offering some level of bespoke services, with meals delivered by dumb waiters and laundry services delivered to the room.

In the 1930s, the idea of collective housing was developed further, especially across Scandinavia. The Kollectivhuis built by architect Sven Makelius in 1935 at John Ericssonsgatan 6 in Stockholm was pioneering new child-rearing techniques that would give working women more options. This unique apartment block offered communal kitchens and creche services,[32] but ended up being popular with an intellectual elite who wanted a place in town. They eventually found the apartments too small and moved into larger homes.

The same fate awaited projects like the Isokon building on Lawn Road in North London. Built in 1934, it was also an example of "convenience" expressed in services first, not in products. Designed by Wells Coates (who later designed the round Ecko radio) for Jack and Molly Pritchard, he focused the design on providing a viable option for busy men and women with professional careers who often only had the choice of bedsits with no private bathrooms and an owner who provided the meals.

In a sense, the Lawn Road flats became an experiment in "Existenzminimum" or minimum viable living, a concept that was the focus of Congrès Internationaux d'Architecture Moderne (CIAM) hosted by Frankfurt am Main in 1929.[33] This event was incidentally attended by Marcel Breuer, who would come to design the furniture for the Lawn Road flats. Wells Coates expressed his design in terms of freedom and mobility.

Our society is above all determined to be free. The love of travel and change, the mobility of the worker himself, grows with every opportunity to indulge it. The "home" is no longer a permanent place from one generation to another...we move away from the old home and family; we get rid of our belongings and make for new exciting freedom. A new freedom which demands a greater comfort and a more perfect order and repose, also a new type of intricacy in the equipment of the dwelling-scene.[34]

Wells Coates and the Pritchards used electricity and the layout of services around the home as an expression of the life lived by a new flexible, affluent workforce. Domesticity as it had been traditionally expressed was secondary, and external services were more important than the fitout of the home.

The Isokon apartments were split between a utilitarian function of living and sleeping and "service" area, which was hidden behind a sliding door or a dressing room, bathroom, and an electric kitchen.

The assumption was of these flats as bachelor/ette pads of sorts for professionals who would spend more of their time out of the home than in. Lighting as well as an electric refrigerator were provided. In the hallway, a hatch would allow meals ordered on an internal phone system to be sent up to the right floor using the service lift. An electric fireplace as well as a wireless radio set and a cocktail cabinet concluded the whole setup.[35]

Not unlike the flats illustrated in in Heath's Robinsons' 1939 "How to Live in a Flat,"[36] the theory was that most people would be doing very minimal cooking in their own kitchens and use a communal kitchen downstairs. This didn't happen, as they continued to cook on the little kitchen they were given, and so the ground floor kitchen was turned into a restaurant and communal bar, which became a big hit with socialites, artists, architects, and even spies of the times.

We will be coming back to these examples later in the book, as they illustrate some of the tensions that technology fails to resolve—mainly the role of authorship and selective privacy in the home. A predictive reliance on others is also often unnatural. Far from being a butler or a servant, a communal experience of home (the restaurant, creche service, laundry) requires a particular frame of mind, or advance planning which one might not be in the mood for. As Sartre said, "Hell is other people," and this might sometimes extend to home technologies.

End Notes

1. Pavillon de L'esprit Nouveau (Fondation Le Corbusier, 2018) http://www.fondationlecorbusier.fr

2. Jean Badovici & Eileen Gray, E-1027: Maison en bord de Mer (Marseille: Imbernon, 2015), p. 15.

3. Jonathan Rees, *Refrigerator*, (New York, NY: Bloomsbury, 2005), p. 40

4. Nancy Carlisle, Melinda Talbot Nasardinov, *America's Kitchens* (Boston, MA: Historic New England, 2008)

5. L'Architecture Vivante: E-1027 Maison en bord de mer, Ibernon, 2006, p. 31

6. Nancy Carlisle, Melinda Talbot Nasardinov, *America's Kitchens* (Boston, MA: Historic New England, 2008) p. 144

7. Brinkman and Van de Vlugt, *The Sonnenfeld House* (Rotterdam: NAi, 2001) p. 89.

8. Vinylmint, History of the Record Industry 1877 — 1920s (2018) https://medium.com/@Vinylmint/history-of-the-record-industry-1877-1920s-48deacb4c4c3

9. Gordon Bussey, Keith Geddes, *The Setmakers* (London: BREMA, 1991), p. 9

10. Gordon Bussey, Keith Geddes, *The Setmakers* (London: BREMA, 1991), p. 10

11. Ian Holdsworth, Plastics, *Social Attitudes & Domestic Product Design* (Plastics Historical Society, 2018) http://plastiquarian.com/?page_id=14332

12. Victoria & Albert Collections, EKCO AC 74 (2018) http://collections.vam.ac.uk/item/O121385/ekco-ac-74-radio-chermayeff-serge/

13. The humble home phone: from 1877 to now (Plusnet blog, 2018) https://community.plus.net/t5/Plusnet-Blogs/The-humble-home-phone-from-1877-to-now/ba-p/1319941

14. Elon University School of Communication, 1870s-1940s Telephone, (2018) http://www.elon.edu/e-web/predictions/150/1870.xhtml

15. Becky Gamester-Newton, *8 things you didn't know about The Phone Book* (History of BT, 2018) http://home.bt.com/news/bt-life/history-of-bt/a-short-history-of-telecommunications-in-the-uk-11363870786446

16. Ericsson, The Bakelite telephone 1931 (Telefonaktiebolaget LM Ericsson and Centre for Business History, 2018) https://www.ericsson.com/en/about-us/history/products/the-telephones/the-bakelite-telephone-1931

17. PC Mag Ecyclopedia, Off Hook, https://www.pcmag.com/encyclopedia/term/48299/off-hook

18. Robert Freshwater, Telephone No. 332 (British Telephones, 2018) http://www.britishtelephones.com/t332.htm

19. Zanotta, Chichibio (2018) http://www.zanotta.it/en/products/Accessories/340_Chichibio.htm

20. Charles O'Connell, Living for Young Homemakers: Telephone bench storage cabinet (New York, NY: Street & Smith,1956) http://3.bp.blogspot.com/-1Ch6c69Kvyo/U74VcXYvuUI/AAAAAAAAGmk/R8VvfU5CYrk/s1600/Nelson.jpg

21. Becky Gamester-Newton, *8 things you didn't know about The Phone Book* (History of BT, 2018) http://home.bt.com/news/bt-life/history-of-bt/8-things-you-didnt-know-about-the-phone-book-11364135332039

22. Ammon Shea, *The phone book: the curious history of the book that everyone uses but no one reads* (New York: Perigee Book, 2010)

23. Philco Big Picture advertisement (2018) http://file.vintageadbrowser.com/l-cdh4kbumxc678o.jpg

24. Gordon Bussey, Keith Geddes, *The Setmakers* (London: BREMA, 1991), p. 217

25. Bruce Norman, *Here's Looking at You*, (London: BBC/RTS), p. 55

26. Gordon Bussey, Keith Geddes, *The Setmakers* (London: BREMA, 1991), p. 217

27. Gordon Bussey, Keith Geddes, *The Setmakers* (London: BREMA, 1991), pp. 224, 311, 312

28. Gordon Bussey, Keith Geddes, *The Setmakers* (London: BREMA, 1991), p. 254

29. Jeanine Poggi, Flashback Friday: TV's first commercial ran 75 years ago today (Adage, 2018) http://adage.com/article/media/flash-back-friday-tv-commercial-ran-75-years-ago-today/304777/

30. The man behind Britain's first ever advert (BBC, 2018) http://www.bbc.com/news/entertainment-arts-34312606

31. Gordon Bussey, Keith Geddes, *The Setmakers* (London: BREMA, 1991), p. 326

32. Dick Urban Vestbro, From Central kitchen to community co-operation - Development of Collective Housing in Sweden, (Sweden: Royal Institute of Technology)

33. Yannis Tsiomis, Jean C. Haskaris, Les congrès internationaux d'architecture moderne. CIAM 1928-1940 (Paris: Ecole d'architecture de Paris-La Villette, 1987)

34. Elizabeth Darling, *Wells Coates* (London: RIBA 2012), p. 66

35. Elizabeth Darling, *Wells Coates* (London: RIBA 2012), p. 73

36. Elizabeth Darling, *Wells Coates* (London: RIBA 2012), p. 95

CHAPTER 4

Digital Everything

This book starts with the efficient home, and the time-saving home, then the modern home, and with the advent of post-WWII technologies, it was time for the "home of the future." Space exploration and the early days of the computer would make this vision potent to middle class owners and their children, the Baby Boomers—the first generation of children to grow up in front of the television surrounded by the radio and the telephone. The impact of what they saw on television at age 8 or 9 years cannot be underestimated.

Design and advertising started selling to families the home of the future not only in architectural terms but also in terms of new appliances. DisneyWorld in Orlando, Florida opened its doors in 1955, including its famous EPCOT center, which featured a "Home of the Future" designed by MIT's architecture department professors Marvin E. Goody and Richard Hamilton for Monsanto Chemical. This all-plastic, full-scale walk-through model of a home opened to the public in 1957 and received 60,000 visitors each week until it closed in 1967.

It became the first home showcasing novel uses for plastics and new electric appliances such as an electric shaver, a microwave, and plastic furniture and tableware. These high-definition contexts made the "future" seem palpable and exciting.

© Alexandra Deschamps-Sonsino 2018
A. Deschamps-Sonsino, *Smarter Homes*, https://doi.org/10.1007/978-1-4842-3363-4_4

Movies and Television Shows

The home computer first appeared in the television show "The Jetsons." This US children's television series by Hanna Barbera originally ran for three seasons between 1962 and 1963, but reruns continued to be broadcast over the following decades. The computer was set in a futuristic context, for it was already starting to feel real as it appeared in some workplaces and in DisneyWorld.

As presented in the show, the home was a mixture of a console, levers, and technologies that you could say belonged more to the steampunk era. Rosie the Robot was a sort of computer on wheels, taking over the recognized role of the servant. The fact that she iwass a woman robot and not a male butler was in keeping with what middle classes who could afford a television might have experienced previously. It was both forward-looking and nostalgic, which added to its appeal across generations. Of all the Hanna Barbera cartoons, "The Jetsons" continues to be a strong reference for the computer-based future home life.

A year later, Stanley Kubrick's *2001: A Space Odyssey* came out in theaters and presented a different, darker view of computers. This time, a male persona, HAL, was a danger to its masters. Computers might not have been something we could trust after all, but as the setting for 2001 wasn't domestic, its impact was far from negative. Computers couldn't be trusted but they were still impressive and awe-inspiring, part of a near future.

The Year of the Future

In 1967, the year of the Montreal World Expo, a number of companies would create vivid images of what the home of the future could entail, with a new innovative product of the war and space race era: computers.

At once a "secretary, librarian, banker, teacher, medical technician, bridge partner, and all-around servant," the home computer did it all, according to a 1967 Philco-Ford corporation short promotional film for their 75th anniversary.[1]

Teaching machines, online shopping, security cameras, online banking, e-mail, electronic instruments, digital health and in-home body scanning, video conferencing, online weather reports, online games, microwaving, and global travel and 3D television all featured in this 22-minute film.

When the wife had friends over though, she cooked an "old-fashioned" meal by hand. When asked a question about the computer, she responded "I haven't got the faintest notion, it's just too much for your old mother to understand." Philco's history was in battery technology and radios before they started working on military and space contracts in the early 1960s. Through this mixture of high tech and low tech, they presented the tension between the importance of participating in emerging economies tied to post-war industrialization and family values where the woman was still the owner of the home experience. This dual dynamic would, still today, play with the psyche of a household. You could have progress but not social progress. The Summer of Love was around the corner, but in 1967, it was still important for a woman to play the role of the main consumer and curator of home experiences.

Other companies were jumping onto the computing bandwagon, no matter how realistic commercialization was at the time. It was paramount to show visions that were television-friendly and well-designed, visually in keeping with the times.

In March 1967, the CBS News show "21st Century," hosted by Walter Cronkite, was themed: "At Home in 2001." This 25-minute exploration of the future of suburban and urban living featured a mock-up of a home of the future, which was also provided by the Philco-Ford Corporation. The innovations included the microwave, a 3D television, and projected children educational programs.

This segment also included an interview in the home of General Electric employee Charles Crawshaw. He owned at the time a "computerized communication console" with a readjusted menu for the wife, work-related activities for the father, and math puzzles for their children. The "teletypewriter" was placed in the kitchen this time.

In September 1967 technology consultant and journalist Rex Malik installed Europe's first computer terminal in his London home and was featured in the BBC "Tomorrow's World" program. The computer was thought to be useful as a "robot housekeeper crossed with a private secretary"—both female roles of course. The computer features morning reports of the stock market, storing a list of house shopping, printing out the daily diary, and teaching his child how to code. At £30/week per terminal in rental costs, it was not clear if Mr. Malik installed these for the purposes of the BBC show, but they were outside of the common person's budget.

The Philco-Ford Corporation, Crawshaw, and Malik television features show us that there was a very public interest in the future domestic role of the computer.

That level of national exposure was important in slowly preparing people for a world where their home "devices" might evolve and start to resemble the tools they had in their workplace. More streamlined, they could never be confused with furniture, unlike the early days of radio and television. They acted as useful market testing to find out which of the potential applications might become "sticky." Most of this was attempted by trying to manipulate the vocabulary around technology in the home; describing the kitchen as a laboratory; and using terms like "consoles" and "switchboards" to describe what would have been called dials and buttons before. Co-opting the television screen for other applications also seemed a good way of helping households invest in new computer technologies without having to buy an additional display. It made computers easier to integrate, as televisions were still not present in most of the homes of the late 1960s. But people knew about them even if they couldn't afford them.

In 1969, the American retailer Neiman Marcus went as far as offering a $10,000 Honeywell computer to housewives. It included two weeks in learning how to program it.

More than Screens

The television wasn't the only metaphor computers could use.

In 1956, Bell Labs worked on a "picture phone" that would show a caller who was calling. This was meant to resolve the age-old anxiety around the lack of "peep hole" on a telephone. It was not commercialized, as the lack of bandwidth made it uneconomical, but our current caller ID feature is a direct result of these experiments. Decades later Western Electric would attempt this again, "crossing a telephone with a TV set"[2] (Figure 4-1.) but commercially failing again.

Figure 4-1. *Picture phone during the World Fair 1964*

Computers would take some time to really become natural bedfellows with our televisions and therefore earn a space in our homes. Even CEOs of computer companies, like Ken Olson of DEC, claimed "There is no reason for any individual to have a computer in his home."[3] The space for computation was in the workplace or at school. But as with television, entertainment was the gateway.

Playing Games

Games consoles that emerged out of the miniaturization of electronics and the development of the transistor then silicon chips during the 1970s. As arcade games grew out of mainframe computer development into publicly accessible entertainment, just like the phonograph before it, the privatization of that experience would create an enormous games industry. Games consoles like Magnavox Oddyssey (1972) and Home Pong (1975) gave children a role in deciding how to use the television, as they subverted the initial use of the television screen. They would take over and control its content for the first time.

As games consoles were replaced by stand-alone computers in the early 1980s, the arguments for why to buy a home computer that wasn't particularly beautiful nor integrated with its surroundings were reflective of the changing values in the home. People wanted to buy computers because "that's where things were going" and they understood they needed to understand them. They'd been presented with images of home computers since 1967, after all, and after decades, these were finally available and getting less expensive.

The Microwave

The images of the "home of the future" was also shaping non-communication-based innovations. The microwave oven was one such invention, which explains why it continues to appear in various showcases already mentioned. Patented in the United States in 1950 by Percy Spencer, it was commercialized by Marvin Bock and launched as Raytheon's "Amana Radarange" (Figure 4-2.) in 1967.[4]

Figure 4-2. Amana Radarange 1967

An accidental by-product of WWII radar technology, the microwave was initially dismissed because of safety concerns and the replacability of the magnetron unit that only lasted 3 to 6 years.[5] It was also an extremely large appliance to introduce onto a traditional kitchen counter.

In 1975, *Which?*, the United Kingdom's consumer report magazine, concluded that given the price point and the potential for expensive repairs outside the guarantee period, "we don't think most people in their own kitchens would get value for money from one."[6] Price wasn't the only issue.

Growing fears of nuclear power—and by extension radioactivity—during the Cold War meant it was difficult to convince people that microwave ovens were safe. Public information campaigns eventually won households over, and by 1993 over 90% of Americans owned one.[7]

As a tool of the future, the microwave was the epitomy of the housewife's dream: a tool that eliminated all cooking preparation. The home of the future was finally here! All you needed was a bit of countertop space. As a step in home automation, this should have become the standard for all modern homes, but it didn't end up replacing the oven entirely—it just added another option.

Ownership and Authorship

Add a microwave oven to a kitchen and you still have the whole kitchen. Homes never got rid of the whole kitchen range because they had acquired a microwave. In the face of complete reduction of the preparation, most households still chose and choose today to do some manual preparation for meals or rely on takeaways or restaurants, where someone else replaces the home cook but the manual aspect of preparation is maintained and provable.

The microwave is, in a sense, too good at what it does to bring long-term satisfaction. It's too easy, it feels like cheating on generations of cookbooks, dieting, and expectations on how to feed a family well. The fact is that cooking, as an activity, survives on the craftsmanship of the cook. That craftsmanship is one of the selling points of home cooking, as it's an activity that changes depending on who does it. No other act in the home is shaped by its initiator in the same way. Access to materials, knowledge, implements, and time makes the activity vary endlessly, adding a "local texture" to each kitchen and each home. This affects our image and expectation of a "home-cooked meal," which is to say that the components of the meal are known and so is the author. The growth of frozen dinners and any pre-prepared food obfuscates this notion, and new technologies had to deal with this.

The meal replacement milkshake Slimfast (TM) was introduced in 1977 but was never sold to completely replace cooking—just breakfast and lunch.

Recently, Californian company Soylent (TM) tried to go a step further in replacing all cooking, but its appeal was limited to a very particular type of young professional men who, along with paleo diets, decided that what they put in their body was more about the ingredients than the experience.

This principle of holding on to a selection of manual activities in a home where the manual aspect of the activity gives them legitimacy and gives voice to the "author" are important notions to consider when we look at the attempt at new technologies to enter the home space. Interior decor and food preparation are almost the only ways an owner can claim "ownership" and therefore identity-building inside a home. The technologies that are purchased have tended toward uniformity across all homes, especially the devices we have described so far: appliances, televisions, radios, and telephones. They denote access to enough capital to afford them but are not in themselves reflective of their owner's personanality and impact.

Buttons for Everything

The era of TV dinners and microwave meals presented a certain image of the home of the "future." The advent of central heating and air conditioning also helped cut the home off from its immediate surroundings. No matter what the weather outside, the home was dry, warm, or cool, depending on what we wanted. The home became a spaceship within "Spaceship Earth." It could be controlled, activities sped up, and the outside world ignored. All that was left to do was to figure out what to do with a computer at home.

ECHO IV Home Computer

One of the first home computer demos was the 1966 ECHO IV. This was an early computer setup in the home of Jim Sutherland, who was, at the time, an engineer at Westinghouse in Pittsburgh.

ECHO stood for "Electronic Home Computing Operator" and is now part of the Computer History Museum in California. It was initially built using spare parts from a Westinghouse, and the size of the processing unit was 6 feet high, 7 feet wide, and 1.5 feet deep (Figure 4-3) and was installed in the basement (Figure 4-4).

Figure 4-3. *ECHO IV computing unit*

Figure 4-4. *ECHO IV programming unit in the basement*

According to the museum's archive:

"The computer used transistorized NOR (Not-OR) logic elements made by Westinghouse in Buffalo, which had been discarded after the failure of a project. Management wanted to forget about the whole project and dispose of them as quickly as possible. Jim asked for a loan of the core memory system, power supplies, mounting frames, and 120 of the circuit boards, so he could build a home computer. Jim's boss thought that was great idea, and quickly signed a property pass. Jim spent 6 months drawing schematics for the home computer. Wiring the back frames and installing the magnetic core memory system required an additional 6 months, and by 1966, the computer was finished, and running programs".[8]

His wife Ruth, when commenting on the setup as part of a presentation to the American Home Economics Association Convention in Dallas, wrote:

"Jim started talking about the availability of part of an obsolete Westinghouse computer that could be made into a computer for home use. It wasn't long until one wall of the dining room began to fill up with stack after stack of meaningless parts, which I called junk".[9]

This mirrors the early years of radio sets: incomprehensible new technology brought home by (often) husbands. Cables ran from the basement to the different terminal applications. In its final setup, this included a series of binary clocks in most rooms, a TV control keyboard, a typewriter-based interface in the kitchen (Figure 4-5.) to write menus and shopping lists or print out common tasks, a personalizable alarm clock system, stereo music control, and thermostat control. Of course there was a programming console in the basement next to the processor to enable instructions to be both given and created. Although it's not known how long the computer worked for, the media coverage was extensive.

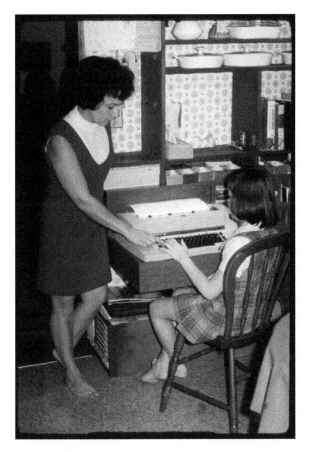

Figure 4-5. *ECHO IV kitchen keyboard being used by the daughter of the household*

In Ruth Sutherland's exposé she described her wishes for such advanced home technology as giving her a sense of accomplishment, relieving her of some more menial tasks and helping educate her children. These themes, expressed in 1966, still come up today. The computer was simply the new recepient of these old desires. The ECHO IV was never commercialized.

A Computer in the Home No Matter What

In a sense, it's surprising that computers did not need to adhere to the rest of the home's visual requirements. Families, after decades of hyberbolic advertising, were ready to invest in computers and to try to find out how they could make their own Jetson's-like reality. Computers could look unique, boxy, unattractive almost; that didn't matter.

As highlighted in Tom Lean's excellent book, *Electronic Dreams*[10]:

"A 1981 survey by consumer guide Which? *found that programming and learning about computers were the most important motivations for buying a micro, far ahead of calculating accounts and playing video games."*

Trying to convince a housewife or children was no longer necessary. The coming age of home computers would yield almost no new ideas about the home in itself, but a whole industry dedicated to the multitude of things you could do with computers. It would lead to the slow death of the radio, the telephone, and the television in their 1950s physical formats. It would disrupt home activities that would have traditionally been associated with the office, like paying bills, booking travel, or making appointments. This was done without the need for companies to talk about the "future of the home."

A vision for a computerized home simply became the vision for the computer in the home.

The television, as a large home screen, wasn't dropped entirely as a medium of communication for digitizing services. The "Viewdata" service Prestel was an early form of internet that worked over the television and the phone line. Launched by the United Kingdom's Post Office in 1979, it gave a person access to a database of consumer information, travel booking, and even online banking. It was eventually sold off to British Telecom and shut down in 1991.

While an important revolution was taking place inside the home, once a place had been made for a computer in the home office, the children's bedroom, or the living room, the rest of the home was left to the whim of interior designers and architects for decades to come.

The Smart House Initiative

How then do we go from the "home of the future" to the smart home? It does not come from the computer sector.

In November 1984, the American National Association of Home Builders (NAHB) organized with a 2-day event organized by the then-president of its research subsidiary, David J. Macfadyen.

A month earlier, the US Congress had passed the National Cooperative Research Act of 1984, which made it easier for competing businesses to collaborate with each other.

With a membership of 100,000 consisting of 50,000 to 60,000 building companies, the NAHB was in a position to get a whole industry (manufacturers, electric and gas companies, trade associations, and government agencies with links to home-building industries) excited about the future of home-building technology. With the home computer entering the market, a different take on technology in the building space was needed.

After attending the Electric Power Research Institute's events, Macfadyen asked his colleague at NAHB, Peiter VanDerWerf, to organize a 2-day event titled "Smart House." The point of the term was to entice people to attend the event, and this was a great success, attracting more than 1,500 attendees.

This was the first use of the term "smart" in a home context.

After the event, appetite for collaborative work around new wiring systems, new types of cabling, and what would eventually be known as "domotics" became a dedicated project that was spun out of NAHB into its own company called SMART HOUSE, LP.

A book was published in 1988 by Ralph Lee Smith[11] documenting the technical underpinnings of the Smart House project. (Figure 4-6.) The introduction is bold in its vision:

"Within ten years after this ground breaking, it is estimated that more than 8 million American and Canadian homes and light-frame buildings will contain intelligent wiring systems. Home devices and appliances will

contain semiconductors—"chips"—that will enable them to communicate with the wiring network, with each other, and with the outside world. Homes will have caught up with nearly everything else in our society that eploys electrical and gas energy—they will become "smart.""

Figure 4-6. *Cover art for Smart House book*

Such was the strength of the term "Smart house," the NAHB trademarked it on October 31, 1984,[12] which might explain why competitors who weren't involved in the work started to use "smart home" as an alternative, more open term.

The objective of the Smart House LP was to make sure new homes could be marketed as being dramatically different from old homes. The objectives of this new company was to move from researching new materials into developing new technologies that could be licensed out to paying partners. The Smart House Inc. company employed 60 people across Bowie, Maryland, Oklahoma, and other sites managed by the partner companies.

The NAHB Research Foundation group bought a 51-acre parcel of land in Bowie, Maryland, a less-developed suburb of Washington, D.C. They would eventually build model homes that were used as a test-bed and collaboration opportunities for 65 manufacturers and 45 gas, telephone, and utilities companies joined the project. Bowie was chosen for its location and the low cost of land at the time.

This process wasn't without tensions in the group, as the gas companies perceived the "smart house" as an all-electric home. The consortium would eventually develop an all-gas test house too to appease those partners. The plans were for a "Smart-ready" system controller and wiring system (all in one house) to be available for sales by October 1991.

By 1990, however, Macfadyen had left Smart House LP., and in 1991 he left NAHB entirely. In 1997, Smart House LP. was dissolved and the assets transferred to a new company, Smart House Inc., which was located in Raleigh, North Carolina and still holds the rights of the trademark; but little else is left of this pioneering project.

The fascinating aspect of the project lies in its inability to see home computers as participants in the "Smart house" vision. They are barely mentioned as stand-alone products that people might have purchased, and instead dedicated wall-mounted touch displays are envisaged (Figure 4-7). "Communicating chips" are mentioned but without much detail and the technical requirements too ambitious. One hundred demonstrator Smart Houses were meant to have been built by 1990, but without an official archive for the project and none remaining today, it's difficult to assess what progress might have been made.

It's unclear what kind of customer would have been able to afford a complete retrofit of their home from the ground up, or how much such a new build might cost.

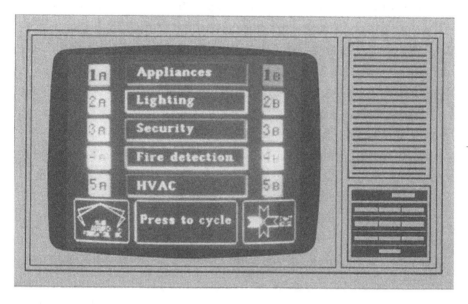

Figure 4-7. Image of touch-display interface

The 1988 book *Smart House* ends with a chapter on the potential applications in a Smart House, and it's almost shocking to see how little has changed since those ideas were put down on paper.

Remote control of appliances for security and safety purposes were mentioned, as well as an acknowledgement of voice interactions and wearable devices for elderly people (Figure 4-8). This was one of the first stabs at addressing future social care issues rather than focusing on able-bodied middle class families with young children. The WWII generation is rapidly aging, and the world is a more dangerous place with conflict diffuse and present in daily life after years of perceived tranquility post WWII.

Figure 4-8. *Scenario for the use of sensors for older people*

They also gave a rather somber vision of home living, one mostly concerned with preventing bad things from happening to people. In a world of computerized interactions that were exciting and fun, it was no wonder the project eventually died. Consumers had, for the past decade, been shown the exciting aspects of computers—not the responsible and practical ones.

Home Robots

Meanwhile, home computers were slowly taking on new forms, not as screen-based interactions like in the Smart House project but as educational toys for children thanks to the growth of academic research in cybernetics and robotics.

An example was the Lectron building block system invented by Georg Franz Greger in 1966, which was sold as a toy.[13] It was eventually manufactured by Braun.

"Robot turtles" were invented by British researcher William Grey in the Walter Burden Neurological Institute in Bristol. In early 1948, he built two turtles to explain how the brain worked, with simple mechanics that were computer-controlled. This was part of early artificial intelligence research.

The Computer Butler

Toys were not the only focus of miniaturized computers. In May 1978, Cyan Engineering, the research arm of Atari, produced a proposal for "Kermit the Robot," which is described in great detail in the book *Atari Inc. Business Is Fun*. The brief from then-CEO Nolan Bushnell to the group was "design a robot that can bring me a beer," recalling earlier visions of computers as servants.

Kermit would speak in "chirps and bleeps" and move around a space, bumping into things on purpose to help build a sense of personality. Due to political turmoil at Cyan, the project never went ahead, but in 1982, two Cyan engineers noted, "A 'vacuum cleaning robot' that Atari could develop and partner with a company like Kenmore to market would be the best way to make home robots a reality." Roomba from iRobot would be launched 20 years later.

By the end of the 1980s, the idea of a "smart home" wasn't popular yet. What did smart mean in the context of NAHB? It implied new building and homes with completely modernized wiring and individually controllable appliances for better elderly living—Not an image that could compete with the excitement of home computers.

That overarching image of a total home redesign was put aside. No great technological consumer home products were launched for the home space for almost 20 years as an entire generation of entrepreneurs and designers occupied themselves with computers and the incoming internet. The excitement of home living had been drained away from the overall home space into a square gray off-white box, It didn't matter where it ended up, as long as it was there. Home computers came to embody accessible future home living.

End Notes

1. Philco Ford, 1999 House of Tomorrow
    (Youtube, 2018) https://www.youtube.com/
    watch?v=TAELQX7EvPo

2. Jim Heimann, The Golden Age of Advertising: the
    60s (Taschen, 2005)

3. Quote Investigator, There is No Reason for Any
    Individual To Have a Computer in Their Home
    (2018) https://quoteinvestigator.com/
    2017/09/14/home-computer/

4. Southwestern Museum of Engineering
    Communications and Computation, Microwave Oven
    (2018) http://www.smecc.org/microwave_oven.htm

5. Southwestern Museum of Engineering
    Communications and Computation, Microwave
    Oven (2018) http://www.smecc.org/
    microwave_oven.htm

6. Helen Leach, Kitchens: the New Zealand Kitchen in
    the 20th Century (Dunedin: Otago University Press,
    2014) p. 241

7. Roberto A. Ferdman, The Slow Death of the
    microwave (Quartz, 2018) https://qz.com/187743/
    the-slow-death-of-the-microwave/

8. Dag Spicer, The Echo Home Computer: 50 years
    later (Computer History Museum, 2018) http://
    www.computerhistory.org/atchm/the-echo-iv-
    home-computer-50-years-later/

9. Ruth Sutherland, Transcript of talk sent to the author (2018).

10. Tom Lean, Electronic Dreams: how 1980s Britain learnt to love the computer (London: Bloomsbury Sigma, 2016), p. 78.

11. Ralph Lee Smith, Smart House: the coming revolution in housing (Columbia, MA: GP Publishing 1988)

12. Smart House, trademark 73618040 filed in the US on January 9th 1986 http://tmsearch.uspto.gov

13. Michael Peters, The Ultimate LECTRON Information Resource and Online Museum (2018) http://lectron.info/#inventor

CHAPTER 5

Cheaper, Embedded and Invisible

From the home of the future to the realities of the home of the late 1990s, there was a gap. The Smart House project wasn't public enough to drive the "smart" revolution yet, but research departments in both academia and large consumer goods companies were. Their impact would start to bring to life examples of connected domestic product experiences that we still hold as examples of the "smart home." Driven by the early days of the internet and its amazing possibilities, computer scientists everywhere started to think about what other devices, other than computers, would be or could be influenced, controlled, or changed by networked information structures. This presupposes that a technically enabled approach is best to create the products of the future, but as we saw, the problems to solve in a domestic landscape do tend to stay the same regardless of the technical advancements. There is, in short, a lack of imagination around the home space in computing circles that is a reflection not only of the people working on these new advancements but of their biases and preconceived ideas of what happens at home.

Introduction

In this chapter we'll explore the landscape of products that started to emerge in the early 2000s where actual product invention was decreasing but 'adding' or 'retro-fitting' an appliance with internet connectivity and

A. Deschamps-Sonsino, *Smarter Homes*, https://doi.org/10.1007/978-1-4842-3363-4_5

its related functions was a new way of selling the smart home. Instead of the radical ask of reburbishing a whole home, innovation was about incrementally adding 'smartness'. This approach was perfect for a growing software industry which promotes 'always in beta' attitudes. Products which were smaller, appliances, furniture, could be embedded with new capabilities and changes could be easily made fot the newest version. A software-led approach to industrial design which was extending away from just home computers felt like a natural progression for the home. Open source software, open source hardware led in turn to open source product design and even open source buildings. The home became a software project and just like software, it was embedded and invisible. Not only this but the departments which were involved in designing these new products were no longer seeped in a culture of product design but a culture of computer science. This meant a re-interpretation of the ways in which design could take its place in the home. But this did not necessarily lead to better product experiences. As we'll see, the motivations for many of the products of the early 2000s and even today continue to come from the same root as the early days of electricity. The messages are often the same, even if technically, things have changed. From the home as a factory to the home as convenience, the smart home doesn't necessarily suggest radically different ways of living and existing through new products or new buildings. It does however suggest new relations to power, data and attention within households and society which we'll address here and in the coming chapters. We start, however before The Smart House project, in the history of computer science research.

Human Computer Interactions

As home computers were becoming ubiquitous, a community of reseachers were exploring new ways in which the miniaturization of the computer might lead to a new breed of products to be developed. This community, although not initially focused on the home space, would end up creating tools that would take the computer into the very appliances and home products that had remained untouched since the late 1950s.

The idea of a smart home that was an all-encompassing change that one would make to a home—updating the wiring, introducing new cabling, living with a heavily predetermined set of automated behavior and relationships—was changed into a piecemeal experience, one appliance at a time. These appliances were developed not by the same researchers but by a new breed of entrepreneurs supported by new tools we will explore later in this chapter.

In the late 1990s, the field of what had been called "Human Computer Interaction" was concerned with the impact of "user-centered" experiences on how computer-based systems developed. Put another way, how computer systems should be designed to be used more easily. In 1996, Xerox Parc researcher Mark Weiser published a number of papers and articles on what he called "ubiquitous computing" and "calm technology." Describing the "smart house" in an article,[1] he talked of how we might interact not just with one computer but a series of embedded computers:

> *Dwelling with computers, they become part of the informing environment, like weather, like street sounds. A house that is true to its house nature must have a certain quiet, even stolidness. Through a thousand subtle cues, computers will help turn our houses into homes. [...]*
>
> *We become smarter as we put our roots deeper into what is around us. The house of the future will become one giant connection to the world—quietly and unobtrusively, as naturally as we know it is raining, or cold, or that someone is up before us in the kitchen making breakfast.*

The use-cases here for what to do with a computer in the home are constantly repeating themselves and are the same as the early computer examples of the last chapter. The question has become not so much about the "why" but the "how." The technical means have superseded the relationship to the "user" or homeowner. When dealing with such an exciting

83

tool like the computer, researchers forget to worry about what they are selling, to whom, and why. This can be easily forgiven seeing as the reason behind pure research is to explore the unknown. The trouble is in the case of the home, the application of technology can influence behavior, social expectation, and relationships. It isn't in itself an apolitical space. Cheaper and smaller technology doesn't translate into "more useful" for homeowners.

"Ubicomp," as ubiquitous computing would be known, is another term that developed in academic circles but did not translate into consumer-facing marketing materials.

In parallel to computer scientists, architects and designers were examining what the impact of computers might be on the act of designing a home. Institutions like the MIT Media Lab and the Architectural Association hosted some of leading conversations about the changing role of a designer in the act of developing new cities, buildings, and homes. For a more detailed breakdown of those pioneers, we recommend *Architectural Intelligence* by Molly Steenson and John Frazer's *An Evolutionary Architecture* in 1997 which both offer great insights in the anxieties of the design sector with computer-aided design in the mix.

Known as CAD (computer-aided design), the idea of designing things using a computer came hand-in-hand with new tools for manufacturing. Computer-controlled manufacturing (also referred to as CNC, SLS, and 3D printing) came in to replace more manual and expensive manufacturing processes. Rather than considering the potential for new technologies on the ways people lived, most designers and architects concentrated on what new shapes could be produced by these new tools. The most well-known of these designers is Karim Rashid, who by 2003 was known for not physically prototyping anything but relying solely on CAD.[4]

Conferences also developed specifically to address this new world of designing with new tools. Two of these events remain today and are still very popular in research communities: Special Interest Group on Computer GRAPHics and Interactive Techniques (SIGGRAPH; since 1974) and the Conference on Human Factors and Computer Systems (CHI; since 1982).

After ubiquitous computing, "calm computing" and "slow technology" were coined by researchers at Carnegie Mellon University.[6]

The authors of this concept, Lars Hallnas and Johan Redstrom,[7] explore computers through the lens of the home. A home space is sold as requiring a degree of "calmness and relaxation that leads to thinking about products without displays that are viewed as taxing and cognitively tiring for a homeowner. Objects and how they are handled act as control mechanisms for digital interactions and are meant to help a homeowner manage decision-making in a rapidly overwhelming information landscape."

Their work comes at a point where another word is emerging in research. The field of interaction design is developing thanks to the likes of former Xerox Parc researchers Bill Verplank[8] and Bill Moggridge and in the UK Gillian Crampton Smith.

A more commercially focused child of HCI research, interaction design, develops in the early 2000s as a dedicated graduate program around the world. Graduate students would go on to work in technology companies more than they would work in traditional design or architectural firms. Well-respected programs include ITP at Tisch School of the Arts[2] (United States), Simon Fraser School of Interactive Arts and Technology (Canada)[3], Rhode Island School of Design (United States), Umea School of Interaction Design (Sweden), the Royal College of Arts Design Interactions (London) and the Interaction Design Institute Ivrea (now defunct).

Contexts that the students were exploring included using the home as a backdrop to new ways ways of dealing with masses of information. The home was often seen as "slow" and quiet, requiring one be shielded away from the growing impact of mass communication. The home was treated by these students as a space to be left relatively or still be made to feel "untouched."

An example is Dario Buzzini's Not So White Walls project from 2004 (Figure 5-1) where text messages appear on the surface of the wallpaper, fading away after a few minutes. The homeowner owns a mobile phone but in the context of them relaxing, the walls of the home dampen the experience to make it apparently more relaxing to absorb the information.

Figure 5-1. *Dario Buzzini's Not So White Walls*

This an ironic point of view considering how much technology had gone into the home at that stage and how much effort had already gone into introducing technology in the home. Students in the early 2000s are of course surrounded by more mobile technologies like early mobile phones and Walkmans. Technology has become about liberation and movement as expressed by Apple's famous ad campaign. The home feels like an antiquated space in comparison for these talented young designers.

As Ed van Hinte put it in his contribution to 'The Responsible Object"[4]:

Currently the future doesn't hold a strong position in the minds of designers and architects. Most of them are involved in reuse of what is already there.

For interaction designers of the early 2000s, the last time the home had been a source of excitement for the future was the 1950 to 1960s. Projects like Richard Buckminster Fuller's low-cost, "packable" housing with his geodesic domes and Dymaxion house are still powerful visual references.

Unlike industrial designers of the turn of the century, who concerned themselves mostly with variations on the blueprint offered by the typical 1980s home, the home was there to be redesigned for the interaction designer, a blank slate. This wasn't the industrial designer's fault, as they focused on learning the new CAD tools that architects were using and were dealing with a large star system with a high profile. The last contribution to the home that an industrial designer had made was Otl Aicher in his 1982 publication "A Kitchen is for Cooking," where the "kitchen island" was introduced.

Incremental change, mostly material- and color-based, was fueling the industrial design sector, which developed an important and imposing star system in the late 1990s. Philip Stark, Karim Rashid, Ross Lovegrove, and Marc Newson were among the designers focusing on consumer products, interiors, and occasionally architectural projects. The tone for turn of the millenium aesthetics was set by Apple's iMac, which launched in 1998. During the launch address[5] CEO Steve Jobs said, "We are targeting this for the number one use that consumers tell us they want a computer for which is to get on the internet, simply and fast."

For industrial designers of the 1990s, design as art was a more provocative and emotive conversation than design as an ally of technology. Many industrial designers in corporate settings saw their role as more important than their engineering colleagues, as it ultimately was the driver of sales. Design as an extension of the marketing department wasn't a popular idea but the commercial imperatives of a product drove its redesign efforts.

In architectural circles, between the 1970s and early 1990s, some architects contributed to the development of many computing paradigms, structures of programming languages, and much more. Their work was covered by Molly Steenson's book *Architectural Intelligence: How Designers and Architects Created the Digital Landscape*[6] and featured the contribution to computer science development of some key architects like Cedric Price, Christopher Alexander, Richard Saul Wurman, and Nicholas Negroponte and the MIT Architecture Machine Group (1967–1985).

In his seminal 1994 book *Being Digital*,[7] Negroponte predicted a scenario for the future of computing, using the home as a metaphor. The scenario was familiar:

If you were to hire household staff to cook, clean, drive, stoke the fire, and answer the door, can you imagine suggesting that they not talk to each other, not see what each other is doing, not coordinate their functions?

By contrast, when these functions are embodied in machines, we are perfectly prepared to isolate each function and allow it to stand alone. Right now, a vacuum cleaner, an automobile, a doorbell, a refrigerator, and a heating system are closed, special-purpose systems whose designers made no effort to have them intercommunicate.

The closest we get to coordinated behavior in appliances is embedding digital clocks in a large number of them.

We try to synchronize some functions with digital time but for the most part end up with a collection of whimpering machines, whose flashing 12:00 is like a small cry to "please make me just a little bit more intelligent."

Machines need to talk easily to one another in order to better serve people.

In a 2003 article by online magazine *TechNewsWorld*,[8] the smart home was updated in a different way:

The general goal of the smart-home movement is to use networking technology to integrate the devices, appliances and services found in homes so that the entire domestic living space can be controlled centrally or remotely.

These two statements illustrate an evolving concept of the home. The mission as it was was to make the home in the image of the models of networking that developed in computing. The hub and spoke model, the nodes in a network, these are all mathematical, wiring, and then computing metaphors used to build computer networks. And they are being used as a blueprint for thinking about activities in the home space regardless of how people actually live. The idea of the network is stronger than what makes the network in itself. In this systematic view of the home, people become actors in a system, appliances and objects become nodes to read information from or control, and routines become time-stamped events to monitor.

The home becomes a computer model to make more and more "understandable" and computationally modeled. Furthermore, if microchips are going to be the future and their ubiquity is undeniable, it is worth looking at what is in the home to find out where they can be put to good use.

As soon as the Smart House project closed in 1997, computing pioneers stepped in offering analogous solutions.

Domotics and Home Automation

Outside of the United Kingdom and United States, other countries were developing their own terminology and markets around home automation. Domotics (or "domotique" in French) developed actively in France. The word domotique was added to the Larousse dictionary and described coming from the latin "domus" and "informatique" or a mashup of home and computing. It was coined in 1982by Marc Humbert, professor at the Universite de Rennes.

Que sais-je? La domotique was a book published in 1988 by Pierre Brun and Edmond Antoine Decamps. It described roughly the same principles expressed by the Smart House project of 1987 and even mentioned audio commands, giving the home a voice (unlike Amazon's Alexa, which mostly gets you to talk to your home).

Domotics is described in this book as the "fourth dimension of architecture," implying that the architect should be the one to push this onto homeowners. Projects like the HD 2000, a connected home on the campus of Rennes University in Brittany were built and then closed in 2000. The then popular Minitel (France's answer to the internet) was also featured heavily.

Much domotic development focused on small, local, and fairly simple automation (the light comes on when you open a cupboard), security camera systems, and automated garage door openers. Often offered as a suite of similar-looking gray or sand-colored boxes, they would be installed for a household by a specialist, either an immediate representative of the company or an electrician. This approach did not vary much throughout the 1980 through 1990s.

The IBM Home Director was another such example. A complete home wiring system with sensors across the home was launched in 1998.[9] It's unclear how successful it was, but its infomercial[10] encouraged home buyers to "create a foundation for the information age in your home."

Most households didn't want to completely rewire their homes for limited perceived value. Computers were enough of a social signal that the "information age" was being embraced by a household, and internet connectivity didn't require a whole new home, just a home router and a 2-hour installation. The Smart House vision required completely new plugs and wiring. Hardly the stuff of middle class households and why a new approach would be needed.

"The cost of installation ranges from $750 to $1,500," Raschke said, "when installed in new homes. Once installed, the homeowner pays standard Internet, cable, and telephone service fees."[11]

If an "all or nothing" approach wasn't going to work, then perhaps a "bit by bit" approach would—an approach that would cater to the rapidly expanding number of people specializing in computer networks.

The idea of cheaply accessible "smart homes" started to circulate and DIY-focused books emerged in the spring of 1999 like *Smart Homes for Dummies*[12] and *Home Automation and Wiring*.[13] Perhaps the whole point of the smart home was that it was something you were going to have to build for yourself after all and not contract out to someone.

The Internet of Things

In 1999, Kevin Ashton, a British researcher, wrote a paper for Proctor and Gamble[14] using the title "The Internet of Things." Written in the context of building information around supply chain by using RFID technologies, this term would soon be used as a catch-all for the miniaturization of electronics into everyday objects.

If we had computers that knew everything there was to know about things—using data they gathered without any help from us—we would be able to track and count everything, and greatly reduce waste, loss and cost. We would know when things needed replacing, repairing or recalling, and whether they were fresh or past their best.

This was an industrial-based approach, but other types of researchers were listening.

In the early 2000s, there was an explosion of research work and academic conferences focused on exploring what internet connectivity in the home might entail. Some of these included:

- Workshop on smart spaces (1999) hosted by the Defense Advanced Research Projects Agency (DARPA), the National Science Foundation (NSF) and the National Institute of Standards and Technology (NIST)[15]

- IEEE conference on Pervasive Computing and Communications (2003)[16]

- Smart Object conference (2003)

- International Workshop on Networked Sensing Systems (2004)[17]

- Multimedia, Distributed, Cooperative and Mobile conference (2005)[18]

- Testbeds and Research Infrastructures for the Development of Networks and Communities (2005)[19]

Many of these conferences no longer exist or were one-off events that led to other more prominent events such as CHI, SIGGRAPH, and IxDa. Beyond the technical lingo, what's important to realize is that the home, closed environments, and networks were competing for research attention internationally.

The refrigerator was only the beginning, as companies invested in new products that could take advantage of miniaturization. Most likely influenced by the rise of computer games that took on more robotic qualities like the Tamagochi (1996) and the Furby (1998), in 1999Sony's Computer Science Laboratory invested in developing Aibo, a robotic dog. Equipped with some simple color and face recognition software, it was meant to play a central role in children's lives at home by 2010. Described as an "entertainment robot," its definition borrowed from the language of hi-fi systems as the television tried to align itself with furniture. Aesthetically, Aibo could be marketed as both an extension of the home computer (made even more exciting by the iMac G3 in 1998), a television/hifi system, and a toy. A total of 150,000[20] units were sold over the 7 years of the life of the first version (a new version was announced in 2017).

Figure 5-2. *Aibo or Sony ERS-110*

Another important group was Philips's Eindhoven research division. They built HomeLab,[21] which opened in 2002[22] and was delivering ideas such as smart picture frames, voice-triggered television interactions, and video calling.

What's clear about this is that a screen-based interaction (with or without stylus pens) is at the heart of this new paradigm of living with computers. We are no longer going to change the structure of the home itself, nor try to design furniture that accomodates new behaviors but simply take advantage of the television, a computer screen, and any available vertical surface (a picture frame, a mirror, a refrigerator) to create completely new interactions and new behaviors. Built on top of MIT's AI Lab project Oxygen,[23] most of HomeLab's products were never commercialized.

Other parts of the business that were more design-led produced future home ideas (not commercial products) seemingly for marketing purposes, such as the Philips Design Probes initiative[24].

The CEO of Philips Design Stefano Marzano worked with well-respected designers Clive van Heerden and Jack Mama[25] as well as Nancy Tilbury, producing projects that touched on the new worlds of wearable technologies, home robots, and sustainable ways of designing kitchens, bathrooms, and more. None of these projects were commercialized. Marzano also wrote *The New Everyday: Visions of Ambient Intelligence* in 2003, giving a voice to ideas of technologies in the home space. The work done in the Design division was clearly very different from what HomeLab concerned itself with. A tension between a computer science and user research-led approach and a design-led approach was clear through the work, and much of both types of research are no longer part of the Philips agenda, as it started to shed and sell off various divisions in 2013.[26]

The work of Philips illustrated a growing schism at the turn of this century between a computer-centric view of what is possible and what is desirable in the home space, heavily influenced by what was technically possible. The ideas were incrementally innovative, thus more palpable or acceptable and therefore more dull. The excitement of the 1950s was gone, and the computer's view of home living ruled.

The primary outcome of HomeLab seems to have been the Living Light concept,[27] which was commercialized as Ambilight. A backlighting for television, the colors of which would dynamically change according to what was being shown, it could hardly be considered radical. But this incremental change was easier to commercialize more quickly and is still on sale today.

In comparison, the work produced by Philips Design was so far away from being produced but inspirational enough to fulfill the needs of a marketing department keen to position the company as a leading voice for the future of home living. It was in keeping with some of the computer-aided design fantasies created by the Karim Rashid showcased in design shows and the the growing sector of contemporary design magazines such as Wallpaper*, I-D, and others.

This tension between a computer science approach to the home and a design approach wasn't unique to Philips. We've chosen to mention them as most of their work was open and well-disseminated. They represent most large consumer-facing companies that struggled to bring together technology and engineering focused talent in the same room as designers. From the ideas shown in the last 15 years by Philips, smart mirrors and frames are still around in the collective research imagination, and some have even moved into the market. This is rare. History is littered with research ideas that were never produced for a future home that is yet to materialize.

Away from the research labs, new ideas were emerging around not only the home but also product design.

Open Source and Open Design

As the home computing revolution developed, a new generation of professionals (mainly software developers) brought their politics to work.

The open source software movement has a history worth diving into but we won't cover it here. It's simply important to think about it as a branch of software development that advocated for work to be shared, amendable, and publicly disclosed for a large number of people to help support it, applying the sociological principles of "many eyes" to a project. The more people have access to the inner workings of a project, the more people can contribute to its maintenance. These principles were developed in the 1960s, as computers and coding was developing and bugs needed to be fixed.

In 2001, the Creative Commons project was founded and applied the ideas of open source to help creatives (especially photographers) share their work, retain recognition for the work, and limit repeat use under some circumstances. A non-profit organization, their mission is described as:

> *Creative Commons helps you legally share your knowledge and creativity to build a more equitable, accessible, and inno-vative world. We unlock the full potential of the internet to drive a new era of development, growth and productivity.*[28]

What is the relationship between these software and digital projects and the home? The link was made in 2005 by Israeli designer Ronan Kardushin,[29] whose masters thesis project included publishing the manufacturing files necessary to make his furniture designs (Figure 5-3). Referring to his work as "Open Design," he produced work that was specifically aimed at traditional product designers with the aim of making the designs downloadable, modifiable and open to replication by others.

Figure 5-3. *Ronan Kadushin's Open Design furniture*

In 2010 he published the Open Design Manifesto,[30] which took some of the more socialist sentiments of open source software and tried to apply them to the act of furniture-making. Far from a 1960s-fueled critique of capitalism, Kadushin acknowledged that authorship and licensing remained important to the world of design, a key difference with software. Designers want consumers to know who is the original designer.

A new product and services market is a natural outcome of a network of designers, manufacturers, consumers, and retailers using a common pool of open designs.

The designer should always be acknowledged as the original creator and owner of the design, even in case of a derivative design. If an open design is produced for commercial use, the designer has to agree for such use and get paid.

The physical world and the objects with which we surround ourselves were perceived as coming from the same act of creativity as software. This wasn't the case of course, and the effort was short-lived but perfectly captured in *Open Design Now*,[31] a book published in 2011 by the Dutch Waag Society.

This idea of open source software-fueled product design even extended to architecture with the Wikihouse project that started the same year. The Wikihouse project described itself as:

> *an open source project to reinvent the way we make homes. It is being developed by architects, designers, engineers, inventors, manufacturers and builders, collaborating to develop the best, simplest, most sustainable, high-performance building technologies, which anyone can use and improve. Our aim is for these technologies to become new industry standards; the bricks and mortar of the digital age.*

This is the clearest statement of intent around making the home an extension of the digital world, as if one was really completely capable of absorbing the other.

Wikihouse works as a digital library of files you can download, send to a local manufacturer with a CNC machine (computer-aided cutting machine), and assemble the frame yourself. Many temporary structures were set up for various events and festivals around the world.[32]

Only one housing structure was commissioned by a couple in England.[33] Motivated by the shortage of locally made bricks, UK-based Martin and Janet Mobbs decided to look for alternatives for their "agricultural worker's dwelling."

After seeing the TED talk from Alastair Parvin, the founder of Wikihouse, they reached out to him. Alastair grew up nearby, and his firm Architecture 00 was contracted to help design a two-story version of the Wikihouse files for their land in the Midlands near Coventry.

It took 2 weeks to raise the structure, with the help of local friends, and 4 years until they were able to live in their home. The plumbing and electric systems were not planned into the original design, requiring Wikihouse to collaborate with the Mobbs to amend the design as they went.

The advantage of the project was the close relationship to the founders and their skill set, regardless of how open source the project was.

The Wikihouse Farmhouse (Figure 5-4) was an example of a great collaboration between the owners and the architects, facilitated by digital tools, but that relationship was still expressed in on-site visits and much patience from the owners who saw it as a labor of love, working toward a house in which they could spend the rest of their days. The fact that the project was open source was almost secondary to the relationship and the ability for Wikihouse to learn from a client's actual experience of building with a digital structure. This experience was also shared with others. No open source files would ever help with the realities of installation or maintenance of a home in this case.

Figure 5-4. *Wikihouse Farmhouse construction site*

The idea that sharing something on the internet is enough illustrates a reality constructed by a culture of CAD and not a culture of manufacturing realities.

More recently a new project called the Open Building Institute seems to have taken up where the Wikihouse left off[34] and has been building a home in parts since 2013, documenting the tools they have used on a "library"[35] of parts. This isn't for the faint-hearted, and 100 people were involved in the various efforts.

The objectives of working at this scale are unclear. By using open and documented processes and tools, the process becomes slower and more involved, and many more people are needed to get a basic home. Who is this for? It's a noble set of technology principles applied to the highly proprietary world of construction machinery, but unless there is streamlining and mass adoption, it is likely to suffer the same fate as the 1997 Smart House project. Trying to rethink and redesign a home from the ground up, literally, is for the wealthy with enough time, land, or staff on their hands.

As the computer took over the means of production in product design, the limitation of real materials and the commercial realities of building homes became less accessible and fundamentally understandable to design professionals. Until it is as easy to order as a prefabricated home from a catalog, the world of open source homes will remain a very hard, expensive dream only the few can afford.

Rethinking Appliances

While considering the whole of the home and how difficult it was to sell, companies around the world were also concentrating on applicances as lower hanging fruits to develop. Research laboratories were looking to revamp home appliances with the combination of computers, early internet, and e-mail. The refrigerator became an unlikely candidate for this emmerging approach. As such this kitchen appliance hadn't changed significantly in engineering terms since the 1950s but had evolved in its capacity and design. It became larger, double-doored, and presented an 'empty surface' to take advantage of in a world where surfaces were rapidly becoming screens and touch tablets. It became the first victim of an appliance-centric view of internet technologies.

Why the refrigerator? Part of this can be explained by the 1921 expression "The kitchen is the heart of the home" Coined in a *Ladies Home Journal* article, "The Disappearing Kitchen Range,"[36] it was in fact used to offer a critical view on home efficiency. It was so catchy people use it still today—both to justify the awkward position of the kitchen as we talked about in the last chapter but also as an excuse to constantly focus and spend money on the most energy-demanding area of the home.

Most kitchen appliances will take decades before they are replaced so homeowners need to be lobbied for decades before making a new purchase. This is ideal for research and development departments tasked with blue-sky thinking as there is little pressure to develop immediately commercializable opportunities.

In 2000, appliance manufacturer LG launched its Internet Digital DIOS fridge (Figure 5-5), which had been under development since 1997. Technical capabilities included:

- TFT-LCD (thin-film transistor-liquid crystal display) screen with TV access

- Local Area Network (LAN) port

- an electronic pen

- data memo

- video messaging

- schedule management functions

- a webcam used as a scanner tracking what is inside the refrigerator

- an MP3 player

The refrigerator also provided home owners with information such as:

- the inside temperature

- the freshness of stored foods

- nutritional information and recipe suggestions

In addition, the electricity consumption was half the level of conventional refrigerators and the noise level was only 23 decibels.

Developed in Korea, LG Electronics (the division that developed the refrigerator) had submitted 75 patents[37] associated with the development of this product. Described as a "digital refrigerator," the language points to the term "smart" not being exactly mainstream. When interviewed,

Young H. Kim, President of the Middle Eastern and African Operations for LG, wrote:

> *This is the first time moving image communications technology, previously only available in multi-media products, has been used in a home appliance. [...] The refrigerator has been transformed from a mere electronic appliance for storing food, to a total family entertainment and communications centre.*[38]

Figure 5-5. *LG DIOS R-S73CT the first smart fridge*

This is a choice of words that has aged badly, but the fridge as an obsession for redesign remains. Left alone for more than 80 years, its large unadulterated surface seemed to attract what can sometimes be described as "feature creep" in the early 2000s. Documented beautifully on the blog[39] 'Fuck Yeah Internet Fridge' written by UK technologist Roo Reynolds, LG's attempt wasn't the last and hundreds of smart fridges have since entered the market, working on the long game of convincing someone that their next purchase will include internet capability. Although not necessarily commercialy successful LG had thrown down the gauntlet and the rest of the home and all its appliances were opened to redesign.

The Arduino

In as much as retrofitting a product with new technologies was emerging, a community of non-professionals would also start to 'hack' commercial appliances to subvert their initial use. While the ideas of open source were not necessarily very successful in the architectural space, another area would take better advantage of the nascent industry of "open source hardware." Hardware in this instance indicated electronics rather than planks of wood.

In 2003, in Northern Italy, things were afoot in the unlikely world of design education. Far from being a computer science-based graduate program, the Interaction Design Institute Ivrea was a privately funded post-graduate interaction design program with a small cohort of 15 to 20 students in a 2-year program. Hernando Barragán's 2003 thesis project was a more accessible electronics prototyping platform: Wiring.[40]

Wiring is both a programming environment and an electronics prototyping input/output board for exploring the electronic arts and tangible media. It can also be used to teach and learn computer programming and prototyping with electronics. It illustrates the concept of programming with electronics and the physical realm of hardware control which are necessary to explore physical interaction design and tangible media aspects in the design discipline. [...] It will enable users to quickly prototype their ideas and concepts in the physical world, allowing users to concentrate on the quality of their designs, the interaction, ideas, or concepts being illustrated, rather than concentrate on showing that the technology works.

The project was interesting to some of the staff who, through a process that is still disputed,[41] developed their own version. They called it Arduino (Figure 5-6), the name of a former King of Italy and the local bar where staff and students would end up at the end of the day.

Figure 5-6. *Arduino Serial in 2005*

The Arduino's innovation was that it was cheap and easier to learn than what was available to computer science students at the time. For 15 Euros ($20) a design student could design a new product with electronics in it.

First manufactured in Italy in 2005, manufacturing premises opened elsewhere, and its access increased year on year. This helped grow what was to be known for years as the "Maker movement" as the Arduino was put in the hands of design students, hobbyists and tinkerers, researchers inside large corporations, and finally budding entrepreneurs.

At first the recipients of an Arduino might build something simple for a student assignement or on the weekend. Many shared their work online, taking the open source approach a step further to share project pictures, the code used to program the Arduino, and a list of parts. Resources and events like Instructables, Make Magazine, and Maker Faires contributed to the increase in exposure of the Arduino to a growing global community.

What did people build? Anything on which you could put an Arduino and exploit its computing capabilites. A connected cat door, SMS-based notifications for your plants, whatever an inquisitive mind could think of, an Arduino could be used to prototype it.

This was so different from how product design was usually developed because its basis was not on invention from the top down but took an existing product that could be "hacked" to augment or change its original function.

A solo project made on a weekend doesn't make an industry, however, and in 2009 when the crowdfunding online platform Kickstarter launched, funding became more easily accessible. Now, not only could anyone access the tools of invention cheaply but they could also finance their project in a way previously inaccessible.

This unlocked an entire industry, as it gave investors some metrics to look at to gage consumer appetite for a product. If a team made something that could seem attractive enough to a few thousand people on a crowd-funding site, they could invest with more confidence, especially if the product was for consumers. Consumer-facing products was not a traditional space for venture capitalists or angel investors. Websites, management software, and mobile apps were more popular with investors, so crowd funding allowed investors to get excited by more physical products.

New and inventive products from teams with experience of mass manufacturing or even product design was a completely new proposition, and the pool of ideas seemed endless. The smart watch dreamed up in the 1946 "Dick Tracy" comic strips was made real through a $10.2M campaign by Pebble in 2012.[42] It was one of the most funded projects on Kickstarter.[43] Larger manufacturers followed, improved on Pebble's groundbreaking work, and eventually drove them out of business.

The new world of connected products was clearly acceptable to consumers in ways they hadn't been before.

The increase in Wi-fi adoption in homes, as well as the smartphone evolution, contributed to this. Computers were getting added to phones and walkmans were transitioning to phones, so consumers were getting used to the merging of previously separate devices into one. Why wouldn't a computer or even a phone merge with lamps, lightbulbs, thermostats, or anything else really?

A Cornucopia of Ideas

In this section we review the home and the recent history of appliances and connected home product development room by room. This isn't meant to be a complete review of everything on the market now but will showcase the amount of products that have been commercialized over the past 10 years.

We also look at some of the early failures and challenges that have had an impact on product development more recently. It's important to also keep in mind that this is a landscape of entrepreneurship that is shifting both geographically and across time.

Governments around the world might at some point or another assign various pieces of public funding or other forms of support (grants, incubators, events, and training) dedicated to physical product-focused businesses. This might in turn create an environment where a certain type of product is in development for a period of time, but when support is stopped, those companies are left to their own devices. The journey of entrepreneurship in the home-connected product world isn't easy. Early pioneers like Ambient Devices (United States) and Violet (France) were succeeded by many start-ups. Sometimes products were developed by small teams in dedicated accelerators and incubators. These, in turn, provided much larger businesses with the market test and inspiration for their next line of products. Other times, a design company would instigate the development of a new connected product working with an expert from the growing Arduino community or its successors (e.g., Raspberry Pi). In all of these cases, success is not guaranteed, as selling the promise of a smart home on the basis of a single new product interaction remains an elusive goal.

Living Room

Many objects can be said to belong to the living room. We've chosen just a few different products here to talk about convivial, possibly more community-based emerging product experiences than can be seen elsewhere in the home.

Picture Frames

Wi-fi-enabled picture frames were developed initially in research departments like Philips HomeLab. They came into the market in the form of picture frames you could e-mail a photo to, and then larger picture frames were developed as displays for curated and dynamically changing contemporary art such as Electric Objects (2014) and, more recently, Meural. As one of the cheaper products to connect and the closest to a television or a computer in terms of manufacturing, digital picture frames were one of the first connected objects to suffer from poor digital security. In 2010, Kodak famously assigned e-mail addresses for each of their Kodak Pulse frames. These were taken over by basic spam/phishing attacks, making the product unusable for days.[44]

Radios

Digital radios have benefited the least from internet connectivity. In the United Kingdom, the largest network of DAB (digital audio broadcasting) radios, transmitters, and networks is still not today in a position to switch off FM transmitters. Like a refrigerator or an oven, a radio is a purchase that is not often made, and as radio functions are integrated into mobile phones and laptops, a dedicated radio or radio alarm clock is still a viable market. This is an interesting example of the "limits" of behavioral change and connectivity. The radio network is still very important to many in terms of cheap and universal access to information about the state of the world, and any add-ons are seen as superfluous.

Its minimum viable function of the radio is dependent on a network of content provision that caters to the most basic technology. Depending on where the radio lives in a home, it can act as a "companion" to many living alone, which is demonstrated in the United Kingdom's Ofcom 2017 report on Radio consumption.[45] It also allows this companionship to take place at the same time as other household activities, such as cleaning, cooking, and washing.

According to the Rajar Midas Winter 2017 survey,[46] 83% of live radio in the United Kingdom is still consumed on either an FM or DAB radio. Furthermore, 60% of "catchup radio" consumption is done in the home. These numbers point to a tradition around the use of both the device and the activity that computing has not yet disrupted, unlike the consumption of music in general, which the "boombox" and the Walkman obviously took outside of the home. Homeowners still have habits that are hard to disrupt, either because of local culture or a lifetime of inspiration through marketing messages, films, and general culture.

Sound Systems

Bolstered by the development of mobile phones and bluetooth technology in the early 2000s, the idea of a remotely accessible speaker that now seems so natural originally didn't have its place in the living room.

Now mostly referred to as "wireless speaker systems," multiple speakers are sold to offer high sound quality across the entire home using a Bluetooth or Wi-fi connection to a mobile phone that acts as the "remote." This process of branding speakers as part of a system has made it more attractive to buy more than one, giving a household the idea that they are buying into a family of device experiences. The living room isn't the heart of music enjoyment anymore with this disaggregated listening experience.

The design pioneers of the speaker world, like Bang and Olufsen, were not the first players in this space. Just like the rest of these traditional businesses, the innovation came from newer companies with less of a history in the space.

Bluetooth sound systems were pioneered by mp3 companies like Creative with the ZiiSound D5.[47] This was a new way of connecting with the then ubiquitous iPod without needing to "dock it." Sonos launched its first product in 2005 and has continued to be a market leader, while more traditional hi-fi system companies have been playing catch up.

Speaker technology has now underpinned a recent generation of so-called "Assistants," which are speaker/microphones with an "always-on" cloud service working in the background. These assistive voice-enabled services take advantage of speech-to-text and text-to-speech technologies that had been developing since the 1980s. These are now cheap enough to integrate in speakers, many of them being cylindrical, which is one of the cheapest shapes to manufacture at scale.

These speakers aren't of course strictly speakers and only enable a household to control music and media-based interactions. They are meant as an extension of the household upkeep. A digital servant, they help homeowners remember things for later, shop on e-commerce sites, schedule alarms, and order car-sharing services. Alexa, Amazon's pioneering speaker, is only a few years old, and its hands-free and, more importantly, device-free interactions have delighted many busy parents with young children. Its always-on service does require homeowners to trust Amazon with their ambiantly gathered information: noise level, number of rooms, brand of appliances, shopping choices, and brand allegiances. This is complicated territory in terms of privacy and what policy-makers in Europe call "informed consent." If things happen automatically, away from a screen-based digital interface or interaction, who is in charge? How can a consumer be in complete control of what happens to the information gathered? Most of the assistive speakers do little voice recognition, so children can order items on their own. This is bound to have an effect on children's perception of money, time, access, and work.

The impact of these new technologies is difficult to assess from where we stand today, but it's inevitable that they will have an impact on how the home interacts with city services and commerce. If the living room was made private by the front door, the smart speaker opens that door once more to a world of commerce that is just a whisper away.

These speakers have made many draw parallels with *Farenheit 451*, *Brave New World*, and *1984*, but these novels were written at a time when capitalism was in its infancy.

In a time where the home space plays an active nationally sanctioned economic role (the consumer price index was developed after WWII), we can see the smart speaker as supporting a frictionless experience of retail, making sure the home is as economically productive as it can possibly be when the traditional high street experience is getting less exciting.

Televisions

Much like the radios in our homes, television went digital starting with the introduction of digital terrestrial broadcasting in 1998 in the United Kingdom. Only a handful of countries (North Korea, Bosnia and Herzegovina, Togo, Trinidad, and Tobago, to name a few) are left that have not shut down their analog television transmitters.[48] This means most televisions that are commercially available to households are digital and act as larger screens to access digital streaming services, digital radio services, games, app stores, and speakers. The transformation of the television into a general media consumption platform has led to the introduction of portable computer add-ons. Most digital televisions now have cameras and microphones. They are essentially now able to "listen" just like a computer, and facial features of a member of the household can be used to enable certain features. This may sound strange but helps parents control the type of content a child has access to because the camera "sees" who is sat in front of it.

This is really a television taking on the types of protection that online services have enabled since the beginning of the internet. Controlling access to restricted content is possible online with "SafeSearch" functions on Google and other browsers, but for a television, it was down to parents being present in the home. Now the television can enable that automatically by recognizing the faces of the people in front of it.

These are issues that take time to become mainstream. It was only in 2015 that Samsung's controversial stance on its "listening television"[49] was making headlines, despite the product being launched in 2012.[50] If a household switched on the voice activation function, the microphone would switch on to "listen" for commands but was at the same time sending everything it "heard" to the company and any third parties. This led to Samsung issuing a clarification on its website,[51] but the product is still manufactured today.

Thermostats

The most risky purchase, yet the one with the most commercial success, has been the world of connected thermostats. Using a mobile app, a homeowner can turn on and off the heating in a home. Other functionalities include the thermostat "learning" from the household use. The risk factor is linked to the reliance on a larger infrastructure and also the collective aspect of the experience. How warm you might like your home may clash with your family, so ultimately controlling a collective experience from an individual mobile phone can prove to be tricky. Many companies have developed products that are now available (Echobee, British Gas Hive, and more), but the first actor in this space was Nest. Nest was launched in 2011 by a team of former Apple employees and was eventually acquired by Google in 2014.

Children's bedroom

Putting children to sleep is one of many challenges parents face, and various companies have tried to address this opportunity. Suzy Snooze by BleepBleeps (a UK company) is one of the more elegant solutions with a nightlight and timer. Just like televisions, baby monitors now include cameras and have become more than radio-controlled speakers. By being connected to the internet, they are exposed to security vulnerabilities we know from the world of computers. In 2013, in a high-profile event, a camera-based baby monitor was compromised, letting the hacker speak through it.[52]

Protecting children from harm is obviously a concern in any household. This used to mean preventing them from having access to hot surfaces, drowning in the bath, or putting their fingers where they shouldn't. The world of connected toys both extends the play possibilities but also the risks.

The cost of sensors was for a long time higher than most toy companies were willing to commit to, but this changed recently, and many took risks in introducing computing capabilities in dolls and other toys. A more gentle toy was launched in the United States in 2013 and was called Teddo the Bear. Developed by Green Goose,[53] it was a teddy bear with simple sensors that acted as a controller for a tablet game. By physically moving the toy, the character in the game would physically move too. This simple interaction wasn't technically very complex, using a simple accelerometer to measure movement.

The complexity of toys increased with the same tchnology as smart speakers being put inside dolls. The US-My Friend Cayla doll was banned by the German government in February 2017 as an espionnage device.[54] The same criticiscm was made of Cayla as of Samsung's televisions, but the fact that the target market was children represented a perceived higher risk in a country with very aggressive privacy laws. This has led to European regulators considering a ban of all connected toys and the technology press[55] calling for families to avoid buying these products.

This puts young companies in this sector in an awkward position as the law starts to catch up with technology in the home. Just like the safety laws that govern the manufacturing of products for children in terms of materials, size, and use, the digital life of a toy now matters too to the safety of a child in the twenty-first century.

For infants, though, it seems the digital safety is secondary to the physical safety, as robotic crib Snoo[56] (launched in 2016) and tracking sock Owlet[57] (launched in 2013) have both been relatively successful and have avoided negative press.

Master Bedroom

Sexual activity isn't the first thing you'd think would get connected but the early adopters of health trackers like Fitbit tagged their "performance" on the online graph provided by the online platform, only for that activity to be published publicly on Google in 2011.

In general, the world of remotely connected sex toys has been very successful and can be found in any well-stocked online store or high street shop. Customers in long-distance relationships and with a bit more money will find products that can be controlled remotely for the other person's enjoyment from the comfort of an app. In Western societies that have moved toward apps as a preferred way to engage with future or potential sexual partners, connected sex toys feel like a natural extension, no pun intended.

The more prosaic connected products for the bedroom relate to improving a person's quality of sleep. Connected sleep masks, pillows, mattresses, and lighting promise to create the perfect conditions to help someone with sleep apnea or insomnia. There is rarely scientific research to support the claims made by these products, and because many of them are less than 5 years old, it's hard to get very excited about Wi-fi connectivity flooding the bedroom. In light of recent publications that discourage people from even having phones next to their bed, it's not clear what the future of this particular category might be.

Kitchen

The kitchen is awash with connected product experiences. From the connected refrigerator we have covered before to smart food scales, kitchen gardens, kettles, and more, internet connectivity in the kitchen continues the tradition of wanting to help women save time and energy. The rise of "foodies," television chefs, and workout-oriented diets like "paleo" has increased the marketing potential of kitchen appliances to men as well as women. The kitchen has become more lab-like, and the focus is not on streamlining activities but being "smart" about one's time. The language has changed, as less women are spending their time caring for a home, but the message is more or less the same. Tasks related to cooking can be done more efficiently with the right tool no matter who you are.

The process of integrating connectivity in larger appliances isn't simple and represents for most companies an important risk. A connected oven that loses internet connectivity might pose a risk to a homeowner. A connected washing machine or connected kettle (the most power-hungry product in a home) might have a major economic impact on energy bills if used too often. These considerations have meant that even if the kitchen feels like the natural home of new technology, adoption has been slow and corporate investment slower still. This is also a space where brand trust is very important.

Connected kitchen start-ups tend to be tabletop appliances, as they don't have to compete with larger 50-year-old appliance brands but with narrowly targeted kitchen utencil companies like Starfrit (North America), Joseph Joseph, or Oxo (UK). This may mean that they are more likely to be considered as gadgets rather than products in their own right. If we focus on the developments of kitchen products developed since 2006, the following companies have led the way.

In 2006, Botanicalls[58] was born out of a project at New York's ITP graduate program. The first SMS-based watering system, it allowed you

114

to get text messages when your house plants were drying up. This project led to a plethora of plant-watering systems that used in-soil sensors to measure the level of humidity and alert home owners in a variety of ways, whether that was through audio messages, tweets, or e-mails. Companies like Easybloom,[59] Moistly,[60] Parrot,[61] and Koubachi developed products that broadly offered the same experience. Many of these products are no longer supported or have been discontinued. This led the way for watering systems that were more advanced, and in 2009, the Estonian company Click and Grow was founded.[62] This miniature hydroponic system aimed at growing kitchen herbs isn't strictly connected to the internet. It did give others confidence around that market of foodies who didn't have a garden but wanted to grow their own food.

Recent companies have followed suit with large-ish refrigerator-like appliances that can be controlled or monitored from a mobile app. Changes in marijuana legislation around the world have also been good for these companies. Products like Leaf,[63] CityCrop,[64] Tregren,[65] and Gro[66] vary in size, but all offer the same functionality for herbs of different sizes or sun and watering needs.

On the kitchen counter, we also find more common, less cumbersome products looking to enhance the cooking experience.

The Drop smart food scale was launched in Ireland in 2012. A Bluetooth-enabled food scale connects to a tablet app to help novice cooks prepare meals step by step, visualizing and adjusting the ingredients and quantities dynamically. An analogous system is the Hestan Cue System.[67] An induction ring that is connected via Bluetooth to a pan and a mobile app, it works with bespoke recipes and videos. The temperature of the induction ring is controlled to improve cooking and only works to cook one thing at a time or when living with very limited space in a high-density skyrise. Since the company is based in Hong Kong, that scenario may be realistic for its customers.

In 2013, Smarter, a London-based company, launched iKettle, a mobile-app-controlled kettle. Far from being a flash-in-the-pan gadget, the company has had a lot of success, offering mobile apps to connect coffee machines[68] and a camera[69] to monitor the contents of the refrigerator.

Large, consumer-facing brands have started investing over the last 5 years to augment their product line with a mobile app component. This doesn't mean that the product line is significantly altered or that completely new products have emerged but simply that "put a chip in it" has reached a level of acceptance that makes it easier for large companies to invest.

In 2016, Nespresso launched a connected coffee machine: Prodigio.[70] Bosch even developed a line of connected appliances for the kitchen under one app called Home Connect.[71] This line of products was launched in 2014 and as of this writing includes dishwashers, washing machines, coffee makers, and ovens.

Whirlpool,[72] LG,[73] and GE[74] also offer a similar mobile app to connect to their own products. Others like Samsung are trying to offer connected experiences that will work across other brands, recognizing most people are not that loyal to appliance manufacturers. Their Connect Home[75] (the branding does tend to get repetitive) Wi-fi hub helps connect products across many other companies[76] but not immediate competitors.

This is a problem. Connected experiences in the kitchen rely on most people upgrading their largest appliances or buying compatible products. As of 2010, 57% of UK homes owned a dryer and 40% owned a dishwasher.[77] This is partly due to the size of Victoria housing and the turnover of households.

This means that growing a family of connected products with one brand is unlikely. Many households will hold onto their cooker, oven, or refrigerator for up to 20 years. A connected appliance company must be ready to support a product for 20 years with software updates and technical support. This is rare, and many connected appliances use an app that is out of date with the owner's mobile phone operating system. If it is done at all, it's the type of support structure only large, well-known brands can build.

As mentioned earlier in this section, the connected kitchen experience continues to feed off the same tropes we have described in the earlier parts of this book. The challenges for companies that have invested in connected cooking experiences doesn't come from other appliance manufacturers but from changes in lifestyles of the incoming millenials. More of them live communally in cities or still live with their parents, relying less on the development of skills that a generation ago would have been considered essential to home life and home-making. According to some market research, "People ages 15 to 24 have spent an average of between just 11 and 17 minutes daily on food preparation and clean-up activities."[78]

The popularity of Soylent[79] could be seen as an extreme response to this trend. A lack of interest in complex cooking experience for childless couples or single people will very likely lead to a decrease in engagement in the kitchen as "the heart of the home," and if someone needs an app to boil water, or an industrial robot arm[80] (with Moley from UK-based Moley Robotics) to cook a meal, it probably means they are trying to avoid the kitchen entirely. The lack of servants leads to technologies trying to emulate that now rare (or elitist) role or people changing their habits entirely. An increase in use of home-delivery services is also transforming the experience of eating at home for that demographic.

It's therefore no surprise that most appliance companies tend to aim their marketing efforts at families with children. This market of mid-20s to late 30s affluent professionals is more likely to spend time in their homes, with enough disposable income to invest in reducing the preparation time of meals. This market isn't completely safe for traditional manufacturers though. The likes of Bellota Baby,[81] Ratatouie,[82] and My Mummy Made It[83] are baby and child food-delivery services that are likely to put additional pressure on traditional home cooking, begging the question, "Will we need a kitchen at all in the future?" If we don't, we will have come full circle, back to the home of the late nineteenth century, mostly relying on a city-based food experience, and only having breakfast at home?

Bathroom

We alluded earlier to the work of Philips in influencing the next generation of bathroom experiences with smart mirrors, but the most popular application in this space has been the scales. Initially Wiithings (a French company) developed their Wi-fi Body Scale in 2008 to enable members of a family to track their weight fluctuation over time with a chart on an app. The product would also enable a person to automatically post their weight loss on Twitter.

Wiithings eventually developed a scale aimed at weighing babies at birth, helping parents track their growth.

The French company Kolibree developed a connected toothbrush in early 2014 and funded the manufacturing with a crowd-funding campaign. Using a games metaphor, they sold the toothbrush as an accessory to mobile games. At the end of the same year, Oral-B launched their Pro 6000 model part of the "SmartSeries." A toothbrush with a Bluetooth connection, its accompanying mobile application is meant to help someone pay attention to the parts of the mouth that are getting less attention. Philips waited until 2016 to launch a similar product.

It's no coincidence companies like Oral-B let smaller companies get ahead of them in the smart home space. Buying something totally new from a newcomer is risky and only the so-called "early adopters" are willing to invest. These early adopters help influence a larger proportion of buyers who will eventually make a purchase from a more trusted brand while still feeling they are participating in a "revolution" in the home space. This applies to the whole of the home space, of course, and not only to the bathroom.

In the bathroom space you might now be able to find connected mirrors that act as dashboards, toilet bowls that analyze your excrement, and shower heads that help you save water and money or enable you to control the temperature for your children's shower.

It's true to say these are available and have been commercialized, but that's not to say they are present in most bathrooms yet. These kinds of products tend to be expensive and launched less than 10 years ago; it's still difficult to tell which of them will end up a fixture in the average bathroom like the electric shaver or toothbrush might be.

Consider the fact that the first commercialized (corded) electric toothbrush, the Broxodent, was launched in Switzerland in 1959 and it has yet to appear in the shopping cart that is used in the United Kingdom to calculate inflation nor does it appear in the US Consumer Price Index. The electric shaver, however, does appear. This isn't a perfect method of assessing what becomes "popular" but it does help explain what becomes more standard in people's lives.

There is also the wonderful and murky world of cosmetics and perfumes, which is starting to embrace connectivity. Mobile-app-connected face masks to help manage acne have been some of the more popular applications.

The Amazon Dash, launched in April 2014, enabled households to order consumables with the press of a button (if they had an Amazon Prime account). Unsurprisingly, the most popular ones included toilet paper and other consumables connected to the bathroom.

Entrance

The entrance is a moving feast in a home. From the dedicated japanese 'genkan' to the heat management closed off space for people living in cold countries, it can also completely dissapear to make walking into a home a direct interaction with the living room. The following products fit into this space to bring in some capabilities, especially when it comes to figuring out who is coming in.

Doors

Remote access to one's doorbell or door lock doesn't sound practical, yet to help manage deliveries or control who comes in or out, using a mobile phone is sold as less cumbersome as using a hallway panel or a traditional key. The reliance on stable connectivity is paramount here, and the risk is so high, new connected locks often have a traditional fallback option of a touchpad. Traditional companies like Yale,[84] more established products like August,[85] Ring,[86] and upcoming companies like Ding[87] in the United Kingdom offer the idea of security or what is usually called "access control" using a set of similar technologies. Bluetooth, Wi-fi, and digital video cameras are used across all these companies to enable the mobile phone to become either the digital key or the control unit for access. In the case of Amazon's newest service, Amazon Key, their lock and camera is installed to guarantee access to their drivers for in-home delivery, which is then monitored by the homeowner.[88] This is still the riskiest application of internet-enabled technologies, as opening your front door is a basic requirement of a homeowner. Some homeowners have suffered from a variety of issues[89] ranging from connectivity to low batteries. This explains why Amazon Key installs a keypad lock for access. In this area, the internet connectivity can be seen as an expensive possible hindrance rather than a blessing.

Cameras

Cameras are perhaps one of the oldest commercially successful connected home products, sold as a home security product since the late 1990s as part of a complete domotic installation. The camera technology, as it shrank, was put into dedicated cameras or door-phone entry systems.

They now come with a mobile app so are remotely accessible unlike traditional closed-circuit television systems. The pioneering WeMo camera, the latest Amazon Echo Look that will act as a "style assistant," Nest's indoor and outdoor cameras, and pet cameras at pet height are all examples of the latest options available to consumers. Manufacturers tend to brand these as "smart home cameras." For many consumers, a security camera is often the "gateway drug" to buying other connected products for their home, as the importance of security is high on a household's agenda.

Garage

A North American occurrence more than a European one, the garage door can be seen in some countries as both extra storage space and a way to access a car without having to go outside. Whether it is a question of protecting the car, the owner, or both, the garage has taken on a mythical role in North American culture. First with 1990s "garage bands," then in Silicon Valley's claim that most of its largest businesses were born in garages. This claim and other cultural elements of the garage are explored in *Garage—Hate Suburbia*, a book by Olivia Erlanger and Luis Ortega Govela.[90]

For our purposes we will concentrate on the garage door remote control, which was patented in 1931 but became a commercial success once suburban housing and car ownership increased after WWII. There isn't a lot to connect here (opened or closed) so the level of recent innovation is low. Knowing who is at home isn't necessarily a byproduct of a car being in the garage or not, so over the last 10 years smart locks companies have had more success than connected garage door companies. The Spanish-based HomyHub[91] is one such company and sells itself as a management platform for multiple doors, an extension of a security product. Selling connected parts of a home on the basis of security may appeal to a particular demographic, but many may brush off the risks by investing in a good insurance package. This means that connecting a garage door doesn't become a priority on the list of connected home experience but is nice to have.

Garden

In a similar vein, the garden is a space most of the world's population would consider a luxury and not a chore to be taken care of by a technology service. If it's not taken care of by a paid gardening service, its care is in the hands of a homeowner who actually wants to spend time gardening. The convenience of watering plants remotely or via a mobile app is therefore dubious, as sprinkler systems have existed since the nineteenth century. The 1967 patent for a lawn sprinkler (#3385525A) by Arthur Jacobs remains the predominent design used by most households. Should the need arise to take care of a garden remotely, companies like Gardena[92] have, through mergers and acquisitions, developed a line of soil sensors and sprinkler control systems that can be remotely controlled by a mobile app.

Too Early to Tell?

Many of the products we have mentioned in this last section are not even 5 years old. On this basis and following the laws of most small and medium entreprises, we expect 80% of them will fail. They do represent, however, the change that has taken place between the vision of a smart home in the 1990s, which was about the home as a total system, to now smart products in the home. As connectivity in many Western urban homes can be taken for granted, smart products become more attractive. Move away from the cities, however, and connectivity starts to fail. As most of these products connect a homeowner to an experience that can affect the chances of fires or flooding, if they don't feel confident about connectivity, they will be reticent to invest in making their family dependent on it.

This system versus product view of the home can be seen as diluting the marketing-led 100-year-old image of an understandable, commonly understood and coherent home life. What does a good home life mean in 2018? Is it spending more or less time at home? If anything, the smart home as expressed by product experiences that are controlled remotely hints at a future where the less time we spend at home, the better and the smarter we are. What a departure from the home-bound housewife of the past! The home has become a place of obligations that can be swept aside by the touch of a button or by speaking to the invisible butler of the always-on e-commerce site. Far from being surrounded by screen-based experiences or mechanical contraptions, the mobile phone app has become the command center of home life. In the next chapter, we'll explore future-home-living scenarios, knowing what we know now of the current smart home.

End Notes

1. Mark Weiser, {Open House}, (Xerox Parc, 1996) https://calmtech.com/papers/open-house.html

2. Tisch School of Arts Interactive Telecommunications Program (accessed 2018) http://tisch.nyu.edu/itp

3. Simon Fraser University, School of Interactive Arts and Technology (accessed 2018) http://www.sfu.ca/siat/about.html

4. Paul Rodgers, Megan Strickfaden, The Culture of Design: A Critical Analysis of Contemporary Designers' Identities (2003)

5. The First iMac Introduction (Youtube, accessed 2018) https://www.youtube.com/watch?v=OBHPtoTctDY

6. Molly Steenson (accessed 2018) http://www.girlwonder.com/

7. Nicholas Negroponte, Being Digital (Open Book Systems, accessed 2018) http://archives.obsus.com/obs/english/books/nn/bdcont.htm

8. Gene J. Koprowski, A brilliant future for the Smart Home (Tech News World, accessed 2018) https://www.technewsworld.com/story/31239.html

9.   IBM Delivers Its New Home Director Home Networking System (IBM Newsroom, accessed 2018) https://www-03.ibm.com/press/us/en/pressrelease/2460.wss

10. IBM Home Director (Vimeo, accessed 2018) https://vimeo.com/123332642

11. IBM touts Home Director (c|net, accessed 2018) https://www.cnet.com/news/ibm-touts-home-director/

12. Danny Briere, Pat Hurley, Smart Homes for Dummies (Hoboken, NY: John Wiley and Sons, 1999)

13. James Gerhart, Home Automation & Wiring (New York, NY: McGraw-Hill, 1999)

14. Kevin Ashton, That 'Internet of Things' Thing (RFID Journal, accessed 2018) https://www.rfidjournal.com/articles/view?4986

15. IEEE Personal Communications, Workshop on Smart Spaces (accessed 2018) http://ieeexplore.ieee.org/stamp/stamp.jsp?arnumber=878534

16. IEEE International Conference on Pervasive Computing and Communications (PERCOM) 2003 (accessed 2018) http://www.percom.org/Previous/ST2003/

17. International Workshop on Networked Sensing Systems 2004 (accessed 2018) http://www.ipsj.or.jp/sig/its/maillist/msg00264.html

18. Multimedia, Distributed, Cooperative and Mobile
     Symposium (DICOMO) 2005 (accessed 2018)
     `http://www.dicomo.org/2005/`

19. First International Conference on Testbeds and
     Research Infrastructures for the DEvelopment of
     NeTworks and COMmunities (Tredentcom) 2005
     (accessed 2018) `http://ieeexplore.ieee.org/`
     `stamp/stamp.jsp?tp=&arnumber=1386171`

20. Satō Narumi, Remembering Aibo (Nippon.com,
     accessed 2018) `https://www.nippon.com/en/`
     `views/b00909/`

21. Philips Homelab (Noldus, accessed 2018)
     `http://www.noldus.com/default/philips-homelab`

22. Opening Homelab 2002 by G. Kleisterlee (Youtube,
     accessed 2018) `https://www.youtube.com/`
     `watch?v=n5X1ATmfncs`

23. Project Oxygen (MIT, accessed 2018)
     `http://oxygen.csail.mit.edu/Overview.html`

24. Visions of the future (Philips, accessed 2018)
     `https://www.90yearsofdesign.philips.com/`
     `article/67`

25. vHM Design Futures (accessed 2018)
     `http://www.vhmdesignfutures.com`

26. Philips exists consumer electronics market, (The
     Telegraph, accessed 2018) `http://www.telegraph.`
     `co.uk/technology/news/9836235/Philips-exits-`
     `consumer-electronics-market.html`

27. Boris de Ruyter, Emile Aarts, Panos Markopoulos, Wijnand Ijsselsteijn, Ambient Intelligence research in HomeLab engineering the user experience (accessed 2018) http://boris.borderit.com/docs/engineering_the_user_experience.pdf

28. Creative Commons, https://creativecommons.org/about/

29. Ronen Kadushin, Open Design (accessed 2018) https://www.ronen-kadushin.com/open-design/

30. Ronen Kadushin, Open Design Manifesto (accessed 2018) https://www.ronen-kadushin.com/open-design-manifesto

31. Bas Van Abel, Roel Klaassen, Lucas Evers, Peter Troxler, Open Design Now, Why Design Cannot Remain Exclusive, (Amsterdam, Netherlands: BIS publishers, 2011).

32. Jess Gillespie, Fridaythorpe Shelter (accessed 2018) https://cargocollective.com/jessgillespie/Fridaythorpe-Shelter

33. Janet Mobbs, Wiki Farmhouse (accessed 2018) https://awikifarmhouse.wordpress.com

34. Open Building Institute (accessed 2018) https://www.openbuildinginstitute.org

35. Open Building Institute, Library (accessed 2018) https://www.openbuildinginstitute.org/library/

36. "The Dissapearing Kitchen Range," Ladies Home Journal 38, M.H. Carter, April 1921, p. 96.

37. LG Electronics introduced digital Refrigerator (Appliance Design, accessed 2018) https://www.appliancedesign.com/articles/89516-lg-electronics-introduces-digital-refrigerator

38. LGE to display Internet fridge at Gitex (ITP, accessed 2018) http://www.itp.net/mobile/471462-lge-to-display-internet-fridge-at-gitex

39. Fuck Yeah Internet Fridge (Tumble, accessed 2018) http://fuckyeahinternetfridge.tumblr.com/

40. Hernando Barragan, Wiring: Prototyping Physical Interaction Design (Interaction Design Institute Ivrea, accessed 2018) http://people.interactionivrea.org/h.barragan/thesis/thesis_low_res.pdf

41. Hernando Barragan, The Untold History of Arduino (Github, accessed 2018) https://arduinohistory.github.io

42. Pebble (Kickstarter, accessed 2018) https://www.kickstarter.com/profile/getpebble/created

43. Most funded projects (Kickstarter, accessed 2018) https://www.kickstarter.com/discover/most-funded

44. Kodak Pulse email-to-photo-frame system down for days, millions of memories trapped in the cloud (TechCrunch, accessed 2018) https://www.engadget.com/2010/12/28/kodak-pulse-email-to-photo-frame-system-down-for-days-millions/

45. Communications Market Report 2017, The UK Communications Market: Radio and Audio (Ofcom, accessed 2018) https://www.ofcom.org.uk/__ data/assets/pdf_file/0014/105440/uk-radio-audio.pdf

46. RAJAR Midas Audio Survey (accessed 2018) http://www.rajar.co.uk/docs/news/MIDAS_Winter_2017.pdf

47. TechRadar, Creative ZiiSound D5 (accessed 2018) https://www.techradar.com/reviews/audio-visual/hi-fi-and-audio/audio-systems/creative-ziisound-d5-702310/review

48. Analogue-to-digital TV deadline reached with much work to do (DigitalTVEurope.com, accessed 2018) https://www.digitaltveurope.com/2015/06/17/analogue-to-digital-tv-deadline-reached-with-much-work-to-go/

49. "Not in front of the telly: Warning over 'listening' TV." (BBC, accessed 2018) http://www.bbc.co.uk/news/technology-31296188

50. Gary Merson, Is your TV watching you? Latest models raise concerns. (NBC News, accessed 2018) https://www.nbcnews.com/technology/your-tv-watching-you-latest-models-raise-concerns-483619

51. Samsung Global Privacy Policy - SmartTV Supplement (Samsung, access 2018) http://www.samsung.com/uk/info/privacy-SmartTV/

52. "Texas Couple Nervous After Baby Monitor Hacking", (ABC Blogs, accessed 2018) https://www.yahoo.com/gma/blogs/abc-blogs/houston-couple-nervous-baby-monitor-hacking-171424527.html

53. GreenGoose Interview with Brian Krejcarek (Youtube, accessed 2018) https://www.youtube.com/watch?v=zxnXDOyS_oo

54. Banned in Germany: Kids' Doll Is Labeled Espionage Device," (NPR, February 17th 2017) https://www.npr.org/sections/thetwo-way/2017/02/17/515775874/banned-in-germany-kids-doll-is-labeled-an-espionage-device

55. "Don't Get Your Kid An Internet-Connected Toy," (Wired, December 20th, 2017) https://www.wired.com/story/dont-gift-internet-connected-toys/

56. Snoo (accessed 2018) https://www.happiestbaby.com/pages/snoo

57. Owlet (accessed 2018) https://owletcare.com/

58. Botanicalls (accessed 2018) https://www.botanicalls.com

59. Drew Prindle, Smarten up your garden with these easy-to-install plant sensors (Digital Trends, April 12th 2014) https://www.digitaltrends.com/home/smarten-garden-season-plant-sensors/

60. Julie Strietelmeier, Moistly is a gadget that helps save your leafy friends from a horrible death of dehydration (The Gadgeteer, September 26th 2013)

https://the-gadgeteer.com/2013/09/26/
moistly-is-a-gadget-that-helps-save-your-
leafy-friends-from-a-horrible-death-of-
dehydration/

61. Flower Power, Parrot (accessed 2017) http://
global.parrot.com/au/products/flower-power/

62. The History of Click and Grow, revealed (accessed
2018) https://eu.clickandgrow.com/blogs/
news/18035380-the-history-of-click-grow-
revealed

63. Getleaf (accessed 2017) https://www.getleaf.co/

64. CityCrop (accessed 2017) https://www.citycrop.io/

65. Tregren (accessed 2017) http://tregren.com/

66. Gro (accessed 2017) https://gro.io/

67. Hestancue (accessed 2018) https://www.
hestancue.com/

68. Smarter Coffee (accessed 2017)
https://smarter.am/coffee/

69. Smarter FridgeCam, (accessed 2017)
https://smarter.am/fridgecam/

70. Prodigio, Nespresso (accessed 2017) https://www.
nespresso.com/uk/en/prodigio-machines-range

71. HomeConnect, Bosch Innovations (accessed
2017) http://www.bosch-home.co.uk/bosch-
innovations/homeconnect

72. Whirlpool 6th sense Live app (accessed 2017) http://www.whirlpool.co.uk/world-of-whirlpool/connectivity.content.html

73. LG Thinq (accessed 2017) http://www.lg.com/us/discover/smartthinq/thinq

74. GE Wifi Connect (accessed 2017) http://www.geappliances.com/ge/connected-appliances/

75. SmartThings Wifi (accessed 2017) https://www.samsung.com/us/explore/connect-home/

76. SmartThings (accessed 2018) https://www.smartthings.com/uk/products

77. Association of Manufacturers of Domestic Appliances, Market Information (accessed 2017) https://www.amdea.org.uk/industry-information/market-information/

78. Maria Lamagna, Why millennials don't know how to cook (Market Watch, September 10th 2016) https://www.marketwatch.com/story/why-millennials-dont-know-how-to-cook-2016-08-10

79. Christina Troitino, Soylent debuts strawberry flavour while quietly optimizing for the masses (Forbes, June 28th 2018) https://www.forbes.com/sites/christinatroitino/2018/06/28/soylent-debuts-strawberry-flavor-while-quietly-optimizing-for-the-masses/#1eff16081133

80. Moley (accessed 2017) http://www.moley.com/

81. Bellota Baby (accessed 2017) http://bellotababy.com/

82.   Ratatouie (accessed 2017) http://www.ratatouie.co.uk/

83.   My Mummy Made It (accessed 2017) http://
       mymummymadeit.com/

84.   Conexis L1 Smart Door Lock (Yale, accessed
       2017) https://www.yale.co.uk/en/yale/couk/
       products/smart-living/smart-door-locks/
       conexis-l1-smart-door-lock/

85.   August lock (accessed 2017) http://august.com/

86.   Ring Doorbell (accessed 2017) https://ring.com/

87.   Ding Products (accessed 2017) https://
       dingproducts.com/password

88.   Todd Haselton, Amazon Key changes how
       packages are delivered — just beware of your dog
       (CNBC, November 16th 2017) https://www.cnbc.
       com/2017/11/16/amazon-key-in-home-delivery-
       review.html

89.   August Smart Lock locked me out (Reddit,
       accessed 2017) https://www.reddit.com/r/
       homeautomation/comments/7ecpxe/august_smart_
       lock_locked_me_out/

90.   Olivia Erlanger, Luis Ortega Hate Suburbia, (O32c,
       accessed 2017) https://032c.com/hate-suburbia

91.   Homyhub (accessed 2017) https://homyhub.com/

92.   Gardena, The smart way to garden (accessed 2017)
       https://www.gardena.com/uk/products/smart

CHAPTER 6

Emerging Themes and What's Next?

What of the home in the future then? How will designers, architects, technologists, anthropologists, and politicians imagine us to live? Far from being able to gaze that far ahead in the future, it's clear from the past hundred years that some things may stay the same but be experienced differently. The idea of the home as a private space has been complicated by a variety of "always on" appliances, selling us services instead of products. Middle class and wealthy households in the West might miss the days of in-house servants and emulate their presence by using voice assistants and on-demand services supported by the so-called "gig economy." Cultures are also looking to new technologies to create a collectively agreeable view of what "good" home living entails. We are always trying to get a peek through the curtains and understand how we compare to others when it comes to the ways we live, and new technologies will continue to support home owners in that quest to "keep up with the Jones." We are always on the fence with what we consider to be private.

New technologies continuously enable us to share a common vision and build consensus, while selectively building in privacy. This is a contradiction in terms, one which fuels the technological landscape around us. Our inability to decide between living as a hermit in a cabin in the woods or blogging, lifecasting, and snapping online creates marketable opportunities for the technology sector.

© Alexandra Deschamps-Sonsino 2018
A. Deschamps-Sonsino, *Smarter Homes*, https://doi.org/10.1007/978-1-4842-3363-4_6

Where Do We Get Our Inspiration Now?

Our sources of inspiration have changed with the storytelling means at our industry's disposal. Before the widespread ownership of television, home economics classes, recipe books, magazines, and radio shows would inspire us and tell about what was coming. With television, we could actually see inside another person's home, albeit initially a very beautifully curated home or kitchen. Celebrity chefs like Philip Harben in the 1905s and later the likes of Martha Stewart would pioneer a clean, aspirational way to tell people how to live.

For the more high-brow audiences, UK theater developed the "kitchen sink drama" to reflect on the fact that home living was probably not as pleasant as the world of appliance marketing would have it.

The 1973 American television documentary *The American Family* and the 1974 British show "The Family" started the "reality television" genre. Finally we could see inside more "normal" people's homes and were given permission to snoop around.

MTV's 1992 show "The Real World" and eventually the very successful Dutch show "Big Brother" packaged the experience of home in a more extreme way. The home was a place you had to survive in, stuck with people you didn't know.

Now, the inspiration for future home living is no longer limited to consumptive technologies like radio and television where we don't control the content but is also online, where we look at each other, every day, continuously.

Jeremy Bentham's prison design concept "The Panopticon" (Figure 6-1) was based on the premise that inmates of an institution were observed by a single watchman without the inmates being able to tell whether or not they were being watched. This would keep them in check, as they didn't know if the watchman was there or not.

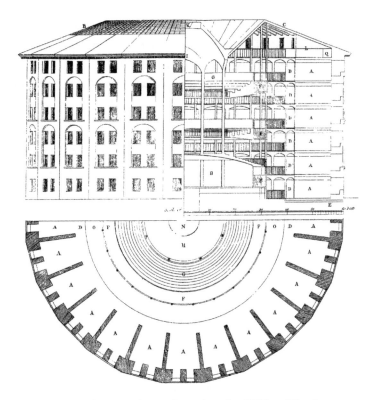

Figure 6-1. *Panopticon prison drawing by Wiley Riveley*

You could say that this is what has happened to the home. Home owners, surrounded by connected everyday products but also their mobile phones, are sharing with others (corporate entities, friends, friends of friends, anyone really) their daily life, without really knowing who is watching them until social media feedback is given (e.g., likes, etc.) or a security breach happens.

We turn to each other for inspiration. Product reviews on Amazon, lifestyle instagram accounts, vlogging—we are each other's inspiration for how to live in our homes. Home-making can become a mosaic image built out of one's television viewing and social media network and can be as real or as artificial as we want to make it.

In this sense we are already living in the public eye, and the home acts as a background to that life, revealing how we live, enabling us to share with others our weight fluctuations on our smart scale, the recipes we have cooked, the amount of sleep we have had, and whether the lights are on or off. We are willing participants in the Panopticonization of our homes.

How might this impact future home living? Stretching the idea of the Panopticon, we might find that our ability to trust strangers with our home-based decisions increases. We might trust a digital service with access to our home camera to establish whether a cleaner is needed or not. We might trust strangers with the decisions around interior decoration, choosing a home to move to, choosing a life partner, or babysitting our children at the last minute as they access all the elements of our lifestyles we're willing to share.

It's not impossible to think that dating mobile apps might even develop based on a profile of use of home objects. Establishing whether someone cooks at home often, watches particular television series, and keeps a home tidy might entice some in starting a conversation.

Looking through someone's wardrobe with a home camera might enable strangers to send shopping recommendations considering the current weight of a homeowner based on their smart scale.

This does not in itself suggest that we would stop owning homes, stop buying furniture, nor stop cooking, but we might do these things even more collectively than we have before. As our level of trust in others has increased in some parts of the digital landscape, the opportunities for traditional robbery have decreased. It's become impossible to dissappear online. Cybercrime and digital identity theft are easier to do online, only sadly without having to go through someone's rubbish, so the risks associated with a more "doors open" policy to home living are likely to increase.

Accessing someone's shed to borrow tools has long been one of the dreams of the service design sector, originally spearheaded by Ezio Manzini, and a more open and collective approach to home living might

136

allow us to have a smart lock on a shed and let others borrow items organically. As companies like IKEA look at more circular ways of engaging with their products, the idea of sharing what's already there is also appealing from an environmental perspective.

Living As a Service

But what happens when home ownership is virtually impossible? Many young people will face an economic environment where owning a home is impossible. Renting may be a lifelong reality for most moving forward. This then pre-supposes that most of the connected products we are developing will continue to be add-ons to a home environment that is layered, multi-use, hard to predict in terms of behavior, and where the romantic ideals of home living take on a completely different life.

Home owners who can't afford the apartment they are in or want extra income already sublet it or parts of it on Airbnb. The "home" experience is commodified using Airbnb, furnishing it with IKEA and taking advantage of tourism and global work practices. In these contexts the most useful connected product has surely been the app-enabled lock, giving remote access to visitors and guests.

Recent articles describe the best smart home technologies to install to give you peace of mind about people staying in your house. Technology has turned homeowners into the watchers in the tower, asking strangers to perform as if they were acting in public.

"Living as a service," "phygital homes," and "living services" have recently become expressions used to describe the return to the service flats of the early 1920s or corporate-serviced apartments. Small rooms with linen and cleaning services, sometimes with en suite bathrooms, sometimes with kitchenettes, communal kitchens, and/or "living rooms" complete this picture, which might as well come from the description of the Isokon building from the 1930s.

Instead of placing this as just another option before having enough capital for a mortgage, this model describes home living to a young person as almost "subscribing" to a home. And these models are, as they were in the 1930s, useful to single young professionals who have just moved into a new city and are looking to meet new people in an environment similar to a college dorm. The question becomes, will this be the only model available to them?

What if future living means never learning how to pay bills, get a mortgage, or wait for an engineer to install your broadband? What would be the consequences of this on future cities? It may mean a complete disruption of the competitive landscape in these baseline services, such as water, energy, broadband, and home insurance. When there is a convenient middleman, there is no way to compete on price anymore, so the service is completely devalued. Future home subscriptions might mean bills are never paid, but services are simply rolled into future home ownership or rental schemes. With the help of connected thermostats, water meters, and energy meters, the average consumption in a home can be calculated and shared with landlords, and a yearly average calculated and rolled into the rent. The management of these services is the premium that people might pay.

This return to a fleeting moment in housing history is also reflection of employment opportunities, demographics, and a willingness on the part of people to explore "minimal living." This trend follows what has been happening in capitals of Asia for decades as documented by Michael Wolff in his "100 x 100" photographs (Figure 6-2).

Figure 6-2. *100 x 100 project by Michael Wolff*

The New Bohemians

Much of the new trends in home living are also a reflection of affluent, often white, middle class, childless people with more capital than their peers and mobile employment, which enables them to build completely different relationships with their homes than parents with young children or a retired person. These new bohemians emulate the 1970s hippy movement without needing to sacrifice on quality of life.

Breather, a Canadian service launched in 2013, wanted to rent out "rooms" by the hour using Lockitron, a mobile phone app enabled lock. Their pitch was to allow you to have some quiet time whenever you wanted it. In a 2014 interview, the founder described the rooms as "spaces where you can take your shoes off." This fits the lifestyle of a young consultant, programmer, or salesperson who travels as part of their work and has shunned traditional hotel experiences, looking for something more flexible and dynamic.

Others, like their predecessors, take to the road. The #vanlife hashtag on social media has also exposed the lives of young people investing in refurnishing a van to retrofit in the resources of a small apartment. A far cry from the disenfranchised poets and artists of the Beat Generation, these often young professionals are willing to go the extra mile to take the experience of home on the road. The willingness to explore how to recreate a home life and the traditional segregation of space in such a small space is impressive.

British technologist Rachel Rayns and her partner built a self-contained van, which they lived in for several months while she took up a post-graduate degree in Scotland. She documented the transformation of the delivery van into a workspace and living space and described what it was like (Figure 6-3).

Figure 6-3. Rachel Rayns's van

She discovered that she'd built a home that needed constant care while being "off-grid." It was "anti-indulgent." She and the van developed a symbiotic relationship built on her keeping things filled, replaced, and recharged. She monitored the weather in the area and looked at the amount of energy she could spend on watching Netflix based on what she had been able to collect that day.

This reliance on energy harvesting had a direct impact on Rayns' daily activities, and she would end up chasing the sun to make sure she had enough to run her heater. She realized that she would have wanted to spend the winter in Portugal or Spain to get enough energy to keep her warm as the days got shorter and less sunny. She would sometimes pay a camping site just to get access to the grid. She described this as "I am not an island," realizing her reliance on larger infrastructure than her own. She also relied on communal, public services such as launderettes and libraries. She used greengrocers to reduce the amount of packaging she brought into the van and went to sports centers or workplace showers when she wanted more than a cursory wash.

When she eventually moved back in an apartment, she realized that she'd lived a lean life in her van. "I have crap everywhere and was much happier with less stuff." She described having the flexibility to go and work from anywhere she wanted.

She reflected on this experience by saying people living in their apartments were living in their own worlds, their own "pods," and were "socially off-grid." Her reliance on others made her feel connected.

Rachel Rayns' experience reflects some of our reflections on the home as contributing to a degree of social isolation as our problems become solvable, not by necessarily interacting with those around us but by purchasing appliances or services from faceless international distributors of fast-moving goods.

Rayns' experience was different from many living in more clement weather, but her ability to realize what she had and what she lost gives us an insight into possible home futures. As climate-change-related displacement starts to affect Western nations, taking a home with you becomes more realistic a notion. This still does mostly apply to single professionals without families but may change with time. Schooling, taxation, and city services may start to develop services for transient, wealthy, middle class, roaming families. The mass introduction of digital tools in education certainly facilitates this scenario but taxation is far from being flexible enough to be "on the go." These new services and attitudes to mobility may offer smarter city councilors and mayors opportunities, but of course the relation to the home is never too far from the relationship someone has with their city or town. Enjoying a home doesn't mean enjoying the city they're in and vice versa. Unlivable or badly managed cities may find themselves being emptied of the precious capital of middle class families if they're able to move about too easily. This is already a problem in rural areas and a more flexible and mobile approach to home living will only exacerbate the problems of rural poverty and sometimes violence. Some kinds of tensions are good, and diversity in communities cannot take place unless people have access to less, not more, choice around home living.

This is of course the rosy side of the financial strain of living in cities where many are pushed into the next best thing to a home: a car. Whether they are college students in the United States or construction workers in Dubai, the car provides the bare minimum that a home offers: locks on doors and shelter. Whether we want to make that financial reality a more "convenienced" market is another question for another book with regards to the kinds of cities that are created by hypermobile poor economic migrants.

The Nagging Home

The home as we have seen has become a breeding ground for a diverse ecology of connected products, smart products, each of them vying for investment and claiming to offer a renewed purpose for a product that most of us have completely forgotten or taken for granted.

This renewed interest in the reinvention of the experiences we have had with 50-year-old inventions hides a more deeply rooted situation.

The smart home of today is also asking us to dedicate our attention away from our work or loved ones to monitor these connected domestic experiences. This creates a relationship that is at best strained and challenging. Why give more attention to a connected kettle and doorbell than to what is in front of us?

The last place we think will "need" us is our own home. We need it more than it should need us, which is what makes it so relaxing. It doesn't need anything from us when we leave it, and it is always there for us to come back to.

We buy insurance and smoke alarms and pay rent and our bills to keep that place "secure" and in a sense "quiet," but we don't necessarily want that same place to contribute to the same stress as our family relations, work, and health might require.

How do we negotiate this tension when the products being designed for us require more than a "buy-and-forget" attitude? Can anyone benefit from this more active cognitive engagement, or is the future of smart homes doomed to a few purchases we will regret later?

Or perhaps the notifications now created by the multiplicity of mobile apps connected to the physical home space create a new landscape of attention and decision-making with which we can distract ourselves, or as Neil Postman would have it, amuse ourselves to death.

Why is the idea of a smart home so potent? Why is technology always trying to reinvent our home experiences? One answer lies partly in the home as a reflection of the self in relation to a larger community. A home and what we put in it that we share helps signal to others that we have "made it" out of our own youth. It is a representation of our modernity, the physical manifestation of us "catching up" with where society seems to be going.

Just as families bought a computer because they had to have one, they might be buying connected appliances, sound systems, and locks because it's just the "thing to do." It is a way of participating proactively in a collective ideal of progress. No matter what's on the news, what is happening politically, or what is going on with climate change, a home is a space one can control—now quite literally with the push of a button.

This is bound to be a passing phase. Just as we take electricity for granted, we may come to take a connected thermostat for granted, displacing our need for modernity elsewhere. Climate change may push us to integrate batteries, solar panels, complex uses of the national grid, very silent washing machines for nighttime use, and others. Reflecting what happened with the radio and the Internet of Things (IoT), kits of solar panels may find their way into people's sheds and office spaces, waiting for cheaper installation or enough installations for them to be taken for granted. The home is a sponge for new technologies—especially if they offer us a way "forward." It is complex deciding who gets to decide which way is forward, but this is bound to be tied with more scarcity rather than more freedom for countries in the West, which have been the focus of the book.

Assistive Technologies

We've also reported on technologies dedicated to making life easier for the "average" homeowner—the average, middle class, Western, able-bodied homeowner. This is hardly a representation of all home experiences, and the area of home automation for the elderly, disabled, and chronically ill is enjoying some well-deserved exposure.

Known initially in the 1950s as "assistive technology," the aim of this area of academic research and product development was to offer disabled people with products that might benefit them at home and out of their home. That choice of language has changed dramatically in the last 10 years to be replaced by the smart home. The UK government even commissioned a report in 2010 on the assistive technology projects that might help homeowners. Titled "Research and Development Work Relating to Assistive Technology 2009-10"[1] the report covers a wide variety of new technologies said to help people with varied disabilities.

Demographically, this will represent the homes of more than a quarter of the United Kingdom's population by 2025 as the world's population as the Baby Boomers retire with a relatively high level of technical literacy.

Stuart Turner,[2] a British computer scientist who also happens to be quadriplegic, has helped large technology companies (including Apple) build better, more accessible open source physical products for the home. His approach is pragmatic and thorough and illustrates the physical challenges in building smart home solutions when the needs of the homeowner and their family are completely different from the average commercial scenario. Adapting these products so that they can be useful to all is a challenge right now. If they're not, they are overcomplicated and meant to be used in such rigid ways as to become useless quickly.

A good example is the area of smart homes for elderly people who are starting to lose some mobility or whose families are starting to worry. Many people over 60 years live on their own and experience social isolation, which leads rapidly to a loss of cognition.[3] Their children who often live away or abroad are currently in the awkward situation of having enough technical literacy to want to help but not living close enough to move in with them.

Smart home solutions offer them a way to temporarily alleviate their guilt, as buying sensors for their aging parents might delay the inevitable (i.e., for them to move back or move their parents in).

The "solutions" or products available for these children of aging parents are problematic at the best of times.

Many solutions focus on tracking a person's position inside the house, their level of exercise, their sleep patterns and helping them in case of a fall. This can be achieved, in principle, with sensors in rooms, bathroom cords, wearable alert pendants, or watches. Companies like Lively (United States) and Kemuri (United Kingdom) developed sensors that tried to disappear from view, attached to drawers or hidden in power sockets. Many academic projects and researchers support this view of elderly care tracking.[4] Not unlike the early all-electric homes, sensor-enabled showcase homes are slowly being shown to both researchers and the general public. The Wintec Interactive Health Village in New Zealand or the Aalst Living Lab in Belgium are some of a growing body of work.

The problem with this approach is that emergency situations happen in such a variety of ways that it's virtually impossible to get the right technology to help unless the home becomes a military zone. At worst, the family of an elderly person becomes a low-level ethnographer, trying to identify "unusual behavior" in their elderly family member and dealing with the stress of plenty of false-positives. This can become more taxing than actually caring for them in person.

This technology-heavy approach has led to much criticism from the design community who see it as using the home to upsell products that benefit no one, or providing very short-lived benefits without adapting to people's real interactions with their homes and environments.

Creative Criticism

The critique of future home living is illustrated in the 2005 video "Uninvited Guests" by design studio Superflux[5] (United Kingdom; Figure 6-4). This speculative scenario features an older man living alone whose family has bought him some tracking devices. A smart fork tracks the calorie content of what he eats. A smart bed alerts him it's time to go to bed.

A smart cane reminds him to walk 10,000 steps a day. These objects nag him into developing coping mechanisms. He buys salad for the fork, gives the cane to a neighborhood kid in exchange for a can of beer, and puts books on his bed. He, in short, doesn't want to be told what to do by well-meaning family via annoying objects. He just wants to watch television.

Figure 6-4. *Uninvited Guests by Superflux*

Superflux are not alone in critiquing the smart home as artists, and creative academics have been the ones to create a non-commercial vision of the future at home. Far from the world of appliance advertisement, their vision of the future smart home can sometimes be dark and dystopian but allows us to isolate problematic behaviors to come.

The Turner prize winning artist Mark Lecky (United Kingdom) took on the smart home in his pieces "GreenScreenRefrigerator" (2010) shown in Figure 6-5 and his book *The Universal Addressability of Dumb* Things[6] (2013).

In "GreenScreenRefrigeratorAction" a Samsung RFG293HABP refrigerator placed in front of a green screen is the subject of a performance that includes images being projected on the green screen, sounds, music, and a "voice" given to the fridge.

This is the description given by the 2011 Transmediale Festival[7] where it was performed:

"In Mark Leckey's GreenScreenRefrigeratorAction, a monolithic black refrigerator stands in front of a green screen, musing upon its own existence. Its monologue, spoken by the artist with a digitally distorted voice, offers observers insights into its thoughts. The fridge describes its daily tasks, gives explanations of itself and its control panels, its outstanding (freezing) properties, and also its cosmological connectedness with things, with the sun, the moon, and the stars. The monologue is based on passages from the holy Mayan book, *Popol Vuh*, a treatise on Marcel Duchamp written by Calvin Tomkins, and fragments from the technical description of the refrigerator. Through an image search, the household appliance attempts to find "friends"—objects that look similar to it. Its search leads to images of black limosines, smartphones, game consoles, and computer cases, as well as the Kaaba of Mecca. The more or less intelligent fridge offers an inkling of what awaits us in the internet of things."

When interviewed about the piece Leckey talked about feeling that connected home products were becoming magical, both in a positive way but also in a more disturbing way. He wanted to react to the fact that contemporary products were becoming black boxes and made people feel like they were constantly in contact with a weird alien object.

Even though they were propelling us in the future, they also paradoxically returned us to the past. Objects were endowed with a spirit of sorts, things had voices which harked back to concepts of atavism, or the idea that traits can reemerge through evolutionary means. There is something more ominous about objects now than there used to be and more anxiety now. At the time, it looked sophisticated, now it looks more sinister.

Domestication and the domestic was confusing for the new father. As a stay-at-home dad, Leckey described being inspired by the objects he had to learn to interact with more, creating a landscape of devices that would color his fatherhood. He felt there was no real language for men, no history of men having their place in the domestic sphere, and no path to success.

Figure 6-5. *Image of GreenScreenRefrigerator (2010)*

What's compelling about Leckey's approach and vision is his breakdown of gender roles and role models to mirror modern family life.

Whether it's stay-at-home fathers, same-sex parents, single parents, or single homeowners, heterosexual couples with children are still at the heart of the marketing message of home living and connected home living. Empty nesters or recently bereaved homeowners might also be made to feel inadequate, as though the possibility of the home is wasted on them. "This home is too big for you" might be uttered. This historical lack of imagination when depicting future home living is bound to be transformed. As family structures change and people live longer in their homes aided by small interactions with technology, the marketing messages they'll receive will change. As advertisers also learn to take advantage of the products people might own, the messaging might change organically with it. The ethnicity and family dynamic portrayed in advertising might be generated based on how many people are, for example, heard interacting in a home with voice assistants. This isn't to say that the solution to a lack of diversity in the smart home of today will be easy to break down but artists like Leckey are able to hold a mirror to an industry that is seeped in 100 years of traditional, Western marketing messaging.

Westley Goatley, another British artist, reflected on the potency of the smart speaker market in his piece "The Dark Age of Connectionism" (Figure 6-6). Based on an Apple Siri virtual assistant asking questions to an Amazon Echo everytime it heard noise, Goatley asked visitors to think about how they triggered and created data, everyday, with something as meaningless as footsteps in a home. The piece asked the audience to think about how they policed their own behavior around these devices whose inner workings were far from a household's understanding of information management and privacy.

This builds an ongoing discourse of investigation into this complex yet deceptively discrete machine. To hear these questions and their answers, audience members must devise ways of being present around the device which do not create more sonic data for it, exploring how such objects in our homes may influence our behaviour if we wish to avoid their listening.

Figure 6-6. *Image of Dark Age of Connectionism (2017)*

Goatley, when pressed to explain his interest in the smart homes, reflected that it echoes the anxiety people have around new technologies and their data-reliant systems. The 2018 scandal around Facebook's relationship with data-based propaganda and "nudge"-based businesses like Cambridge Analytica has exposed commercial dynamics that had remained hitherto hidden from public view. The adage goes, "When the service is free, the product is you," but in the smart home space, the products aren't free.

Digital Responsibility

Not only are they not free, they are often expensive, as companies have to develop complex services that they need to maintain after a household has bought them. After-care in the smart home is more costly than ever to a business. It's one thing offering spare parts for an old washing machine, but making sure that machine's software is always updated and responding to the latest security threats is manpower and work that most traditional manufacturers are not equipped to handle.

If these products aren't expensive, then the company is often choosing to sell them cheaply as the value of the data collected is worth more than the electronics and the plastics combined. The Amazon Alexa, for example, may have been sold or at a loss to make sure it could get more market penetration and its real value researched and extracted after it had become a fixture of the home. When it becomes "part of the furniture" and households find enough functionality to keep it plugged in, but not enough to be suspicious about keeping it plugged in, the real work of data collection happens. Coupled with an app store (or Alexa skills), a speaker becomes a platform for other businesses to extract value from our daily lives.

But isn't that capitalism at work—the extraction of value in every single aspect of the life to turn it over to the market? Well in a traditional capitalist setting, you'd sell someone some soap flakes by appealing to their need to do laundry and protect their family from germs. Now companies are selling a washing machine to a household and then selling the fact that a household does laundry twice a week to someone else entirely. The value chain has expanded away from the household itself.

Not unlike banking, the value is created in a no man's land of abstract concepts like Big Data, profiling, and market research. In short, someone else is benefiting from knowing you do laundry twice a week. You might not know who that person is, but there it is. Does the average home owner care? Mostly they don't, they currently focus on the task at hand, happy with loved ones at home, earning enough to pay the bills, staying healthy, and earning a living. That other people earn a living from the times when they feel the most at ease seems a million miles away from a "wicked problem."

After all, the living room, once made private with the telephone, was made public again by receiving the rest of the world through radios and televisions. Home owners have focused on comfort and how to be at ease and do as little work as possible. People may want to be accompanied by technology that allows them to be themselves. The radio and the television were not "talked to"; information was ready when we were ready to receive it. Then they might login on a home computer when they wanted to. A phone call was made when they wanted to call a loved one. There was a high degree of agency and control of how and when "others" came in and who they interacted with. Now the tables have turned. In a bid for comfort, the modern home owner has let others peer into their lives and make money from them doing very little, collecting energy usage data, the sounds of the television, distracted clicks on a touchscreen.

What else could be captured and exploited in this subconcious capitalism? Micro-movements of the eyes are already captured by laptop cameras, we're bound to see in-home marketing take place as the home becomes yet a new generation of laboratory. Instead of Christine Frederick's Taylorism, it might be our voice assistant or in-home camera that assesses our gait and gives us feedback about our posture. Less of a butler and more of an eager mother, the home of the future may sneak into making us feel like we could improve even the act of relaxing and going to bed. In an aggressively capitalistic environment, everything can be improved.

This new state of affairs has led to many asking "Quis custodiet ipsos custodes?" Who is there to establish what good or bad things are happening to us, our data, without our knowledge? Regulators and governments are responding as the European General Data Protection Regulation[8] came into effect in May 2018 and the IoT Cybersecurity Improvement Act[9] was passed at the federal level in the United States in 2017.

The ethics of organizations that rely on data to operate is, as we saw through Wesley Goatley's work, being discussed publicly. In the United

Kingdom only, there are now think tanks,[10] policy papers,[11] design studios,[12] publicly funded institutions,[13] and academic research departments dedicated to examining the ethical underpinnings of computing. The focus hasn't yet been on the home space, but this is simply a matter of time.

Closing Thoughts

Efforts are already underway to provide end consumers with a degree of reassurance about the products they are going to be introducing in their home. For example, efforts to create certification marks are under way worldwide.[14]

This implies we may end up with home products that are rated according to their "data exhaust" and thus a new generation of interior designers who help us negotiate the tightrope between functionality and a version of privacy. On the other hand, marketplaces currently exist where we can sell our data to the highest bidder. Examples include Wibson, Datum, and Datacoup. Whether the risks associated with the loss of personal data will ever be big enough for consumers to care is unknown. There may be a renewed market for "dumb" appliances for those more nervous about data protection and less worried about energy expenses, for example.

As we've seen in this chapter, the future of home living is as varied as its individual components. Whichever aspect you look at, there are a variety of ways of seeing future scenarios. As each new wave of technology approaches a home owner, we see them behave in the same way as a hundred years ago—tinkering, listening for leading voices to help them make choices, and ultimately getting used to things and moving on to the newest technology. There should be comfort in this.

Consumers are in general more refined in their expectations of new technologies and will come to demand more realistic stories to be told. A family's privacy and the exchange of data against a service will be scrutinized more and more. Young people will also choose not to interact with particular services based on their complexity and their transience.

Broadband providers, energy providers, and the whole ecosystem of appliances manufacturers will have to create richer, more fragmented, and sometimes joint stories about a flexible and smart home living that appeases their uncertainty. Data and how it's handled will become part of the marketing laguage the same way we take energy rating as a given. Home living might become less of a 1950s advert and more of a complex fragmented mosaic, much like life itself.

End Notes

1. Department of Health and Social Care, Research and Development Work relating to assistive technology 2009-2010 (UK Government, October 2009) https://www.gov.uk/government/publications/research-and-development-work-relating-to-assistive-technology-2009-10

2. The ultimate smart home: "Disabled people like good design too," The Times, April 5th 2015. https://www.thetimes.co.uk/article/the-ultimate-smart-home-disabled-people-like-good-design-too-97z5vg3vhtw

3. Jo Cox Commission on Loneliness, Age UK December 2017, p. 8-9 https://www.ageuk.org.uk/globalassets/age-uk/documents/reports-and-publications/reports-and-briefings/active-communities/rb_dec17_jocox_commission_finalreport.pdf

4. SPHERE project (accessed 2017) https://www.irc-sphere.ac.uk

5. Superflux (assessed 2018) http://www.superflux.in

6.   Giulia Smith, The Universal Addressability of Dumb Things, Frieze Issue 155, May 2013 `https://frieze.com/article/universal-addressability-dumb-things`

7.   GreenScreenRefridgeratorAction, Transmediale Archives, 2017, `https://transmediale.de/content/greenscreenrefrigeratoraction`

8.   Regulation (EU) 2016/679 of the European Parliament and of the Council on the protection of natural persons with regard to the processing of personal data and on the free movement of such data, Official Journal of the European Union, 27 April 2016 `https://eur-lex.europa.eu/legal-content/EN/TXT/HTML/?uri=CELEX:32016R0679&from=EN`

9.   Internet of Things (IoT) Cybersecurity Improvement Act of 2017 (Congress.gov, accessed 2017) `https://www.congress.gov/bill/115th-congress/senate-bill/1691/text?format=txt`

10.   doteveryone, (accessed 2018) `https://doteveryone.org.uk`

11.   Data Ethics Framework (Department for Digital Culture Media and Sports, August 30th 2018) `https://www.gov.uk/government/publications/data-ethics-framework/data-ethics-framework`

12.   If (accessed 2018) `https://projectsbyif.com`

13.   Ada Lovelace Institute (accessed 2018) `https://www.adalovelaceinstitute.org`

14.   Open internet of things mark, (accessed 2018) `https://iotmark.wordpress.com/2018/04/27/what-if-open-iotmark-was-open/`

CHAPTER 7

Conclusion

New technologies have shaped not only the way we interact with other family members but the way we interact with our cities. What has been covered in this book mostly relates to a view of technological advancements in the United States and the United Kingdom, two economically prosperous nations. The baseline is high compared to others around the world. We're far from everyone having access to indoor flushing toilets and private rooms for family members, as illustrated by the Organisation for Economic Co-operation and Development (OECD) Better Life Index.[1]

The OECD defines the importance of the home[2] in the following terms:

"Living in satisfactory housing conditions is one of the most important aspects of people's lives. Housing is essential to meet basic needs, such as shelter, but it is not just a question of four walls and a roof. Housing should offer a place to sleep and rest where people feel safe and have privacy and personal space; somewhere they can raise a family. All of these elements help make a house a home. And of course there is the question regarding whether people can afford adequate housing."

The Global System for Mobile Communications Association[3] (GSMA) has established there are more than 4.77 billion mobile phones in the world, which implies that although people's homes might not be up to Western standards, many people are using mobile computing to enhance their home life.

© Alexandra Deschamps-Sonsino 2018
A. Deschamps-Sonsino, *Smarter Homes*, https://doi.org/10.1007/978-1-4842-3363-4_7

Instead of living through 100 years of convincing people to live in particular ways, many are able to organically bring in technology as it applies to their needs, such as safety, belonging, and self-actualization that might have previously come from putting a roof over our heads and is now also brought about by engaging with digital services such as mobile payment systems, social media, and freely accessed information.

This is in sharp contrast with the tools with which nations are measured. The role of the home is still central to the calculation of Gross Domestic Product (GDP), for example. In an agenda of economic growth, the home is the smallest most economically productive unit of a country. The amount spent in a lifetime on products that will be stored, used up, and consumed at home is above any other industry's needs. In the United Kingdom, homeowners now spend more energy than the industrial and services sectors.[4] This fuels the role of technology in the home space. Behind concepts of "time-saving" or making tasks "easier" the manufacturing sector needs the constant stream of sales. The electric iron freed the housewife as much as Alexa frees a parent from spending time shopping. Ultimately, these products encourage a focus on the home space as a factory of activities and expenses that power the economy. We are encouraged to spend more time at home, figuring out new ways to spend less time at home as the home becomes the ultimate engine of a growing digital economy. Shop from home; get a meal from a restaurant delivered to your home; monitor your home remotely; watch opera, theater, or movies from home; rent a home when on holidays; and, finally, sell a home. In the advent of the New York attacks of September 11, 2001, President George Bush's message to continue to spend was a reflection of how much our economy depends on the purchase of goods for the home and home life. Without it, most economies would surely crumble.

Homes are also more and more removed from the ideas of neighborhoods, citizenship, and collective action and participation. As the 50-year anniversary of the May 1968 protests is celebrated across Europe, you could say that the home is the ultimate barrier to political activism.

If every need is fulfilled at a micro-level, it's easier to forget the needs that are not fulfilled at a macro-level and the needs of others who do not share their homes with us. Demonstrating in the street requires us to leave our homes after all.

As political turmoil globally increases and uncertainty rises, we look to the young for ideas on the future. The prospect that most young people cannot afford to own a home or furniture speaks volumes about the upcoming crisis in the world of the smart home. If no one is there to cook, what's a smart kitchen for? If someone's not living at home but renting their home on Airbnb, the amount of money spent on interiors decreases.[5] A young person living in a co-living space doesn't even buy toilet paper. Brand loyalty disappears, and values shift.

The smart home and its vision might become solely targeted at parents and elderly people, the ones that spend the most time at home. A secondary rental market might also emerge for smart home products that can temporarily help families. A smart cot might be helpful for the first few months and sensors for the last months of an ailing parent.

The smart home also started as an infrastructural idea: electricity, gas, and internet. Now it has found its feet at an appliance level: bulbs, thermostats, appliances, and products. The idea of a complete home design may come back as people move to the countryside in search of homes they can afford or want to refurbish themselves. As eco-homes, solar panels, and cob homes come back into fashion, many are finding the idea of re-learning how to make a home interesting. Global initiatives like Cal-Earth (United States), Co-habitat (Poland), Earthships (United States) highlight the housing crisis in many capitals that may unlock a new rural landscape and new types of communities.

Lessons have been learned from 1960s experimental communities like Drop City, and new models of multigenerational living are on the rise. Even architects like Anna Puigjaner of Maio architects in Barcelona are thinking about the importance of community building through communal kitchens,[6] a return to the type of concerns many women scholars have had through the last 100 years.[7]

It's also important to reflect on developments which aren't taking place in the home of the future. The smart home has failed to address some fundamentally troubling effects of the privatization of the human experience. Domestic violence and social isolation of the elderly are two of the most extreme examples.[8] There is currently no home sensor, camera, or speaker that will report a person to the authorities if a woman or child is mistreated inside their home. There is no smart television that will report someone to social care if they spend over 12 hours a day in front of the television. There is currently no smart mirror that will report an instance of self-harm or drug abuse inside a bathroom. We have pockets of public disclosure, but the "sanctity of the home" is still something that is enshrined in law, and in a way dictates what kind of technological solutions we inherit.

Another failure of connected home products has been the provision of product experiences focused on individual users. Switching your lamps on and off remotely when your spouse is still in the house doesn't seem like a great idea. The future of the home is bound to address these teething issues, especially if a newer generation of consumers are more cash-poor. For those living alone at home, connected home experiences can be seen as an attempt to return to a state of childhood where everything was taken care of for us by our parents. Responsibility-free, children are free to enjoy life. As adults, however, many struggle with the management of a home space that is both privately consumed but publicly judged—alone in a home, taking pictures of the parts of it of which they are the proudest, and sharing it online.

People are learning to negotiate the tension between social performance and sharing too much with corporations abroad. A person's whereabouts, behaviors, or their parent's or children's behaviors are there to be traded in for functionality and carefully negotiated[9] in order to regain a sense of control.

The home continues to be a shared fantasy of systems within systems glued together by technological advancements. A constant negotiation of private and public, collective and individual actions, it is bound to seem to endlessly change while its walls stay the same. The change is really experienced in social and economic terms that will constantly evolve. Technology is there to underpin and encourage some behaviors but perhaps not others. The moral value in the technologies that are adopted depends on the household and their own moral compass. A tool, no matter how useful in any given context, is never entirely amoral.

The portrait of the home that was painted in this book is bound to either provoke or offer comfort to designers, technologists, and architects looking to tackle the ideas of smartness in the home. This is a space in which to design carefully, with much respect for the changing economic times that will have more influence than a piece of connected furniture. The fluidity of consumption and precarious nature of politics means people will adapt and find the right technological tools for them at different times in their lives, shaping home experiences that are personal but also expressed collectively. The role of the designer in this space is also to tell stories about home living that feel more inclusive of others around the world as we start to share visions of future home living.

End Notes

1. http://www.oecdbetterlifeindex.org/#/11111111111

2. http://www.oecdbetterlifeindex.org/topics/housing/

3. https://www.gsma.com

4. Energy Consumption in the UK, Department for Business, Energy, and Industrial Strategy, https://assets.publishing.service.gov.uk/government/uploads/system/uploads/attachment_data/file/633503/ECUK_2017.pdf, p.7, 2017

5. Coresight Research, Deep Dive, Millenials and Furniture in the US & UK, Coresight Research, https://www.fungglobalretailtech.com/research/deep-dive-millennials-furniture-us-uk-ten-characteristics-define-market/, Feb 13th 2017

6. https://www.maio-architects.com/project/kitchenless-city/

7. *The Grand Domestic Revolution*, https://mitpress.mit.edu/books/grand-domestic-revolution, MIT Press, 1981.

8. Thermostats, Locks and Lights: Digital Tools for Domestic Abuse https://www.nytimes.com/2018/06/23/technology/smart-home-devices-domestic-abuse.html

9. P.Bihr, M.Thorne, *The Connected Home*, https://theconnectedhome.org/content/connected_literacy.html

Index

A

Access control, 120
Aibo/Sony ERS-110
      (robotic dog), 92–93
Air concerts, 40
Amazon Dash, 119
Amazon's pioneering
      speaker, 109
Ambient Devices, 106
Animal Chemistry (book), 6
Appliances
    blue-sky thinking, 101
    Internet Digital DIOS
      fridge, 101–102
    refrigerator, 100
Arduino
    consumer-facing, 105
    Interaction Design
      Institute Ivrea, 103
    open source
      hardware, 103
    product design, 105
    serial in 2005, 104
    smart watch, 105
    student assignment, 104
    Wi-fi adoption, 106
    wiring, 103
Assistants, 109

B

Bang and Olufsen, 109
Bathroom, 118–119
Bedroom, 113
Being Digital (book), 88
BleepBleeps, 112
Bluetooth sound systems, 109
Broxodent, 119

C

Calm computing, 85
Calm technology, 83
Cameras, 120
Cell-unit, 33
Communal kitchens, 159–160
Computer-aided design
    (CAD), 84, 87
Computer Butler, 78
Computerized communication
    console, 61
Convenience, pleasure and
    collective housing, 53
    companion objects, 46–48
    from efficiency
      to pleasure, 31–32
    freedom and mobility, 53
    hanging up, 43–46

© Alexandra Deschamps-Sonsino 2018
A. Deschamps-Sonsino, *Smarter Homes*, https://doi.org/10.1007/978-1-4842-3363-4